The past thirty years have seen the proliferation of forms of independent cinema that critique the conventions of mass-market commercial movies from within the movie theater. *Avant-Garde Film/Motion Studies* examines fifteen of the most suggestive and useful films from this film tradition: *No. 4 (Bottoms)* by Yoko Ono, *Wavelength* by Michael Snow, *Serene Velocity* by Ernie Gehr, *Print Generation* by J. J. Murphy, *Standard Gauge* by Morgan Fisher, *Zorns Lemma* by Hollis Frampton, *Riddles of the Sphinx* by Laura Mulvey and Peter Wollen, *American Dreams* by James Benning, *The Ties That Bind* by Su Friedrich, *From the Pole to the Equator* by Yervant Gianikian and Angela Ricci Lucchi, *The Carriage Trade* by Warren Sonbert, *Powaqqatsi* by Godfrey Reggio, *Naked Spaces – Living Is Round* by Trinh T. Minh-ha, *Journeys from Berlin/1971* by Yvonne Rainer, and *The Journey* by Peter Watkins. Through in-depth readings of these works, Scott MacDonald takes viewers on a critical circumnavigation of the conventions of moviegoing as seen by filmmakers who have rebelled against the conventions. MacDonald's discussions do not merely analyze the films; they provide a useful, accessible, jargon-free critical apparatus for viewing avant-garde film, which communicates the author's pleasure in exploring "impenetrable" works with students and public audiences.

Avant-Garde Film

CAMBRIDGE FILM CLASSICS

General Editor: Raymond Carney, Boston University

Other books in the series:

Avant-Garde Film

Motion Studies

SCOTT MACDONALD

Utica College of Syracuse University

CAMBRIDGE
UNIVERSITY PRESS

Published by the Press Syndicate of the University of Cambridge
The Pitt Building, Trumpington Street, Cambridge CB2 1RP
40 West 20th Street, New York, NY 10011–4211, USA

© Cambridge University Press 1993

First published 1993

Printed in the United States of America

Library of Congress Cataloging-in-Publication Data
MacDonald, Scott, 1942–
Avant-garde film : motion studies / Scott MacDonald.
p.   cm.
Includes index.
Filmography: p.
ISBN 0–521–38129–0. – ISBN 0–521–38821–X (pbk.)
1. Experimental films – History and criticism.   I. Title.
PN1995.9.E96M33   1992
791.43'75–dc20   92–17446
CIP

A catalog record for this book is available from the British Library.

ISBN 0–521–38129–0 hardback
ISBN 0–521–38821–X paperback

To the hundreds
of Utica College and Hamilton College students
who have shared their reactions and insights with me

Contents

vii

Introduction

The mainstream cinema (and its sibling television) is so fundamental a part of our public and private experiences, that even when filmmakers produce and exhibit alternative cinematic forms, the dominant cinema is implied by the alternatives. If one considers what has come to be called avant-garde film from the point of view of the audience, one confronts an obvious fact.[1] No one – or certainly, almost no one – sees avant-garde films without first having seen mass-market commercial films. In fact, by the time most people see their first avant-garde film, they have already seen hundreds of films in commercial theaters and on television, and their sense of what a movie *is* has been almost indelibly imprinted in their conscious and unconscious minds by their training as children (we learn to appreciate the various forms of popular cinema from our parents, older siblings, and friends) and by the continual reconfirmation of this training during adolescence and adulthood. The earliest most people come in contact with an avant-garde film of any type is probably the mid-to-late teen years (for many people the experience comes later, if at all). The result is that whatever particular manipulations of imagery, sound, and time define these first avant-garde film experiences as alternatives to the commercial cinema are recognizable only because of the conventionalized context viewers have already developed.

Generally, the first response generated by an avant-garde film is, "This isn't a movie," or the more combative, "You call *this* a movie!?" Even the rare, responsive viewer almost inevitably finds the film – whatever its actual length in minutes – "too long." By the time we see our first avant-garde films, we think we know what movies are, we recognize what "everyone" agrees they should be; and we see the new cinematic failures-to-conform as presumptuous refusals to use the cinematic space (the theater, the VCR viewing room) "correctly." If we look carefully at this response, however (here I speak from personal experience, and on the basis of more than twenty years of observing students dealing with their first avant-garde films), we recognize that the obvious anger and frustration are a function of the fact that these films confront us with the necessity of redefining an experience we were sure we understood. We may feel we *know* that these avant-garde films are not movies, but what *are* they? We see them in a theater; they're projected by movie projectors, just as conventional movies are . . . we can see that they *are* movies, even if we "know" they're not. The experience provides us with the opportunity (an opportunity much of our training has taught us to resist) to come to a clearer, more complete understanding of what the cinematic experience actually can be, and what – for all the pleasure and inspiration it may give us – the conventional movie experience is *not*.

These first avant-garde films, in other words, can catalyze what I would like to call our first fully *critical* response to a set of experiences our culture has trained us to enjoy, primarily as a process of unquestioning consumption. I say "fully critical" because the sort of film-critical process I'm describing actually begins the moment we see any form of film that we cannot immediately recognize as a movie, given our previous training. For the generation coming of age in the 1960s, this process often began with foreign commercial features, by Fellini, Bergman, Buñuel, Kurosawa, that did not conform to the expectations we had developed watching Hollywood films. For most people, however, avant-garde films are so entirely unlike "real movies" that they demand a full-scale revaluation of our cinematic preconceptions; they are closer to being "purely" critical.

Obviously, not everyone who has a first experience with an avant-garde film uses the experience as a means of catalyzing thought about Cinema, but for some people, the experience leads them to an extended critique of conventional movie experiences and an awareness that avant-garde film is an ongoing history which has been providing critical alternatives to the mass-market cinema for more than seventy-five years.

The first substantial flowering of avant-garde cinema occurred during the 1920s in Western Europe, most notably in France and Germany, and in the postrevolutionary Soviet Union. In Germany and France, the cinematic apparatus was seen as a tool with which artists working in the fine arts could expand their repertoire, and, by doing so, attract more of the public than visited art galleries and salons. Indeed, filmgoing was becoming so popular among members of all social classes that artists could hope that the expanding audience might embrace visual critique of convention as well as convention itself. The first film Avant-Garde fueled at least two different critical responses to the mass commercial cinema. Not surprisingly, these

2

responses parallel two of the more salient tendencies in the fine arts during the first decades of this century: abstraction and surrealism. Both tendencies resulted in films that were memorable enough to continue to inspire and inform critical filmmaking in Western Europe, North America, Japan, and elsewhere.

One group of filmmakers questioned the commercial cinema's failure to minister directly to spiritual needs in the way music often does and abstract painting was attempting to do. Hans Richter, in *Rhythmus 21* (1921) and *Rhythmus 23* (1923–4); Oskar Fischinger, in his *Wax Experiments* (1921– 6), *R–1. Ein Formspiel* ("R–1. A form play," *c.* 1927), and *Spirals* (*c.* 1926); Walter Ruttmann, in *Opus No. 2* (1922), *Opus No. 3* (1923), and *Opus No. 4* (1923); and Viking Eggeling, in *Diagonale Symphonie* (1924), focused viewers' attention on shape, motion, rhythm, chiaroscuro, and color, in the hope they could touch the spirit more directly than conventional filmmakers did. Related were Dudley Murphy's *Ballet méchanique* (made in 1924 with Fernand Léger and Man Ray), Marcel Duchamp's *Anemic cinéma* (1926), Henri Chomette's *Jeux des reflets et de la vitesse* ("Plays of Reflections and Speed," 1925), and Germaine Dulac's *Disque 957* (1929), all of which foreswore most of the elements of conventional narrative cinema and fore-grounded abstract imagery and rhythms.

The second set of film-critical responses came at the hands of the surre-alists. Using elements of plot, character, and location moviegoers could be expected to recognize, these filmmakers relentlessly undercut the expecta-tions their inclusion of these elements inevitably created, in the hope of depicting and affecting layers of the conscious and unconscious mind too problematic for the commercial cinema. Rene Clair's *Entr'acte* (1924), Man Ray's *L'Etoile de mer* ("Starfish," 1928), and Luis Buñuel and Salvador Dali's *Un Chien andalou* ("An Andalusian Dog," 1929) continually confront one of the central assumptions of conventional cinema: the idea that the individual personality and social and political relations among individuals are basically rational and understandable. These filmmakers were at pains to shatter the complacency created by this assumption. Indeed, since the contemporary mass-market cinema continues to confirm such complacency, most audiences find these particular films – and especially *Un Chien andalou* – as unusual now as when they were made.

In the Soviet Union, the revolution produced a cinema that mounted a direct attack on the mass-entertainment film industry, particularly its func-tion as propagandist for capitalism and the political systems that support it – from a position outside capitalist culture. The major films of Eisenstein, Pudovkin, Dovzhenko, and Vertov combined overt political content and experimental form into impassioned critiques of social conditions and polemics for a more humane political system. Like the films of the first Avant-Garde, the Soviet films may never have been seen by the mass viewing public in the West, but they inspired generations of filmmakers, exhibitors, and viewers, and remain formative influences in various sectors of contemporary cultural life. In Depression America in particular, the result was a Soviet-inspired school of experimental narrative and documentary, perhaps the first American alternative cinema movement.[2]

After World War II, technological and esthetic developments catalyzed a major flowering of avant-garde cinema in the United States. The increasing availability of less-expensive 16mm motion picture cameras and projectors made the production and exhibition of alternative forms of film economically feasible, and it facilitated the development of a broader range of production systems: the less-expensive equipment was accessible to individuals and small groups who might not have found their way into filmmaking otherwise. The smaller gauge also revived the film society movement, which had enlivened the film scene throughout Western Europe in the 1920s and 1930s, offering audiences a broader range of critical alternatives to the economically dominant Hollywood industry. Film societies had been only marginally successful in the United States, largely because of the economic and social power of Hollywood.[3] The availability of 16mm equipment made possible Amos Vogel's Cinema 16 in New York and the nationwide network of film societies it instigated.[4]

The increasingly prolific American alternative film scene took strength from the new prestige of the visual arts, especially in New York. The emergence of the New York School of painting and of generally related developments in experimental music (the increasing prestige and influence of jazz and of John Cage, for example), literature (the New Novel in France, Beat poetry in the United States), and the other arts not only suggested approaches useful to filmmakers looking to provide audiences with alternatives to Hollywood (the gestural emphasis of much abstract expressionist painting, for example, helped to inspire gestural camerawork that tended to give "headaches" to filmgoers weaned on Hollywood movies), it polemicized the excitement of individual self-expression. The motion picture camera offered a way of extending the New York School's commitment to the importance of individual vision (a commitment evident, for instance, in their large-scale canvases), both literally, since the movie screen is a "canvas" of considerable size, and in terms of audience: filmmakers could hope that because of the massive popularity and prestige of the commercial cinema, film-critical alternatives to Hollywood might be of widespread interest.

4

By the 1960s, the cultural critique implicit in all these developments had developed substantial social and political power. Those who had developed a commitment to the ideal of self-expression and to new, critical visions increasingly found themselves confronted by events that confirmed and extended the social and political relevance of this commitment. The struggle for civil rights, the growing resistance to the Vietnam War, and the general reaction to post-World War II repression and conformity were felt and expressed through all the arts. Under severe economic pressure from the growing success of television, even commercial directors were attacking the traditional rhetoric of the Hollywood industry, in an attempt to retrieve the audience. And alternative filmmakers working entirely outside the industry were exploring a variety of new approaches.

The North American avant-garde cinema of the late 1940s, the 1950s, and the 1960s is prolific and diverse, but many films of the period share (almost inevitably overlapping) critical tendencies, general ways of confronting the audience's conventional expectations and demonstrating the limitations of mainstream cinema. These tendencies provide a historical context for the films discussed in this volume. One such tendency is evident in films that focus on the filmmakers' self-revelations. In some cases, these self-revelations are presented symbolically, by the "visionary" filmmakers whose work P. Adams Sitney explores in *Visionary Cinema:* Maya Deren, Kenneth Anger, James Broughton, Sidney Peterson, Stan Brakhage, Gregory Markopoulos, and so on.[5] In other instances, filmmakers present personal revelations quite directly. When viewers see Carolee Schneemann's *Autobiographical Trilogy (Fuses,* 1967; *Plumb Line,* 1971; *Kitch's Last Meal,* 1973–8); Jonas Mekas's *Walden* (1969), *Reminiscences of a Journey to Lithuania* (1972), and *Lost Lost Lost* (1975); Andrew Noren's *Adventures of the Exquisite Corpse: Huge Pupils* (1968, remade 1977); and Robert Huot's *Rolls: 1971* (1972) and *Third One-Year Movie – 1972* (1973), they are in immediate touch with important dimensions of the filmmakers' experiences. These filmmakers demonstrate that there are other interesting, fulfilling ways to live besides the narrow range of middle-class lives (and their predictable "secrets") marketed by so many industry films. And the unusual forms they develop for depicting their experiences reveal the conventionality of industry narrative. The candid revelations of the personal filmmakers provide viewers with a healthier set of personal and filmic options.

A second tendency is exemplified in what has become known as "trash." The films designated by the term develop recognizable narratives, with characters, sets, costumes – all the fundamental elements of Hollywood moviemaking; but either because the filmmakers lack the economic means for achieving industry-level production values, or because of their decision to use their limited resources to affront conventional expectations by painstakingly constructing a trashy look, viewers of trash films are continually aware of the gaps between this rendition of a story and the way the story would be handled by an industry director. The viewing experience becomes a process of recognizing, with more than normal precision, the economic and social requirements for conventional entertainment and the implications of these requirements. Important contributors to this strand of development include George and Mike Kuchar who produced a remarkable series of collaborative films in 8mm from 1957 to 1964, and then developed individual careers in 16mm (and more recently in video), Ken Jacobs (in his early films: *Little Stabs at Happiness,* 1959–63; and *Blonde Cobra,* 1959–63); Jack Smith (in *Flaming Creatures,* 1963); Andy Warhol (in some of his more plot-oriented melodramas); Paul Morrissey (in *Trash,* 1970); and John Waters (from *Hag in a Black Leather Jacket,* 1964, through *Desperate Living,* 1977). The trash films often provided their commentary on conventional movies in exhibition situations that functioned as comments on "normal" moviegoing: They helped to create the Midnight Movie Circuit.[6] Making trash films, exhibiting them, and going to see them was a way of responding to the sanitized, bourgeois worlds created in so many industry melodramas.

For still other filmmakers, the network of avant-garde screening rooms and production facilities was a public arena within which one could engage viewers in an exploration of the nature of visual perception, and thereby reinvigorate perceptual capacities that tended to atrophy in commercial theaters. The preeminent filmmaker here is, of course, Stan Brakhage (he is also seminal in the development of the self-revelatory tendency just described). Brakhage has made hundreds of films, but those that have had the broadest impact over the years (*Window Water Baby Moving,* 1959; *Sirius Remembered,* 1959; *Scenes from under Childhood, No. 1–4,* 1967–70; *The Act of Seeing with One's Own Eyes,* 1971) have focused on the issue of vision and, in particular, on the gap between the world as it is generally constructed for us by the camera and the world as it is apprehended by untutored human vision. For Brakhage, the movie camera and the imagery it normally produces are cultural artifacts developed as a product of Western rationalism; they reconfirm modern society's commitment to a range of visual perception limited by a "practical" view of experience in which the goal of amassing material wealth requires conformity in how we see and how we act. Brakhage's films are often direct assaults on conventionalized

6

vision and on the camera, which Brakhage redirects in the service of un-conditioned sight.[7] Bruce Baillie's films – *Castro Street* (1966), *Tung* (1966), *Quick Billy* (1967–70), *Roslyn Romance* (1978) – are closely related to Brakhage's.

Other filmmakers have explored other dimensions of vision generally ignored by conventional movies. Peter Kubelka (*Arnulf Rainer*, 1960), Tony Conrad (*The Flicker*, 1966), Paul Sharits (*Razor Blades*, 1966; *Ray Gun Virus*, 1968), Taka Iimura (*Shutter*, 1971), and Standish Lawder (*Raindance*, 1972) exploit black and white and color flicker as a means of addressing viewers' retinas and the physiological and psychological mechanisms which transform visual stimulation into consciousness. In the mid-1960s, Andy Warhol used unedited, roll-long shots to achieve a variety of particular effects (in *Sleep, Kiss, Haircut*, and *Blow Job*, 1963; *Empire*, 1964), all of which demanded that viewers confront conventional film-viewing assumptions about the duration necessary for seeing particular visual events. And Andrew Noren in *The Wind Variations* (1968); Larry Gottheim in *Blues* (1969), *Corn* (1970), and *Fog Line* (1970); and Brakhage in *The Text of Light* (1974) discovered remarkable visual worlds in the details of their domestic surroundings.

Although all three of these tendencies have continued to have a significant impact on alternative cinema (and some impact on commercial film), by the end of the 1960s, new developments were resulting in new forms of critical cinema, in which only elements of these particular tendencies remained evident. The arrival of the Baby Boomers at the doors of American educational institutions effected an immense growth in the education industry. For the first time, film history and practice became the subject of widespread academic study. The influx of foreign films into the United States, and the continued development of avant-garde film were helping to convince a new generation of academics that cinema was *worth* studying: These films often revealed a seriousness and a complexity reminiscent of the canon of literary works studied in university literature departments. Further, the profound impact of new European cultural theory in these same institutions was convincing many that, precisely because of its impact on popular thinking, the popular cinema *needed* to be investigated if students were to come to understand how they, and the films they saw, were formed by the culture in which they lived.

The emergence of film as an academically viable subject for investigation provided a new audience for popular and alternative cinema – the college classroom – and created a new interest in aspects of film history and practice generally ignored in popular theaters and, to a lesser degree, in alternative

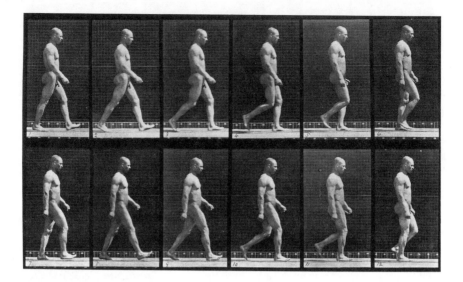

Eadweard Muybridge, *Man Walking at Ordinary Speed*. Courtesy International Museum of Photography at George Eastman House.

screening rooms. These new interests affected film viewers and filmmakers, many of whom studied or taught film in academic contexts. Some of these filmmakers were interested in developing more sustained and systematic critiques of conventional film and television narrative entertainment, and especially in responding to the tendency toward overconsumption marketed by television advertising and confirmed by the visual/auditory overload of a good many alternative films of the 1960s. For them, reattention to cinema's beginnings became a particular source of inspiration. Since modern cinema had supposedly become what it was by leaving the discoveries of the early cinema pioneers behind, filmmakers began to return to these "primitives" to see if what conventional film history had defined as primitive was really a set of less marketable, but still useful alternatives. After all, many of those who were seeing their first avant-garde films in the 1960s, and who were not tuning into them, tended to call the avant-garde films "primitive." Perhaps there was a relationship between what the first pioneers had done, and what the avant-garde "pioneers" were doing.

Avant-garde filmmakers did, indeed, find a resource in what had been called primitive cinema. In some cases, their excitement about what they discovered blinded them to the commercial realities of the early days, but this excitement, whether they explored it directly or whether it formed part

8

Marion Faller/Hollis Frampton, *"782. Apple Advancing [var. 'Northern Spy'],"* from *Sixteen Studies from VEGETABLE LOCOMOTION* (1975).

of a more general environment that had an indirect impact on them, helped to fuel the approaches that are the subject of this volume. For our purposes here, these approaches can be roughly identified with Eadweard Muybridge and the Lumière brothers.

In film historical circles, Muybridge is known for his discovery that motion can be photographically analyzed into component parts and for his construction of the Zoopraxiscope, the combination of the technologies of animation and projection he used to demonstrate that if he resynthesized the various stages of particular motions, he could create the illusion of the original motion the still images represented. Muybridge's extensive "motion studies" have been seen as an important stage in the move from the animation of drawings, which characterized the popular "philosophic toys" of the nineteenth century (the Phenakistascope, the Zoetrope), to the printing of photographs of stages of motion on strips of celluloid; and the Zoopraxiscope is usually considered an important early stage of the movie projector.

The aspect of Muybridge's work that is most interesting for the films I'll be discussing in this volume, however, has to do with the information he used his technology to discover, and the way in which this information was presented. In order to document his motion studies so that viewers would be able to measure the type and amount of motion accomplished during any fraction of a second by one of the humans or animals he photographed, Muybridge mounted a linear grid behind his subjects. And in order to make possible the precise comparison of one phase of a given motion to another phase, he mounted the photographs of particular phases of motion, recorded at evenly spaced intervals of time, in a grid. (Often a given motion was photographed from multiple camera angles; phases of the motion, taken from the various angles, were mounted on grids within a single frame: This way the differences in a particular movement evident from differing angles could be explored.) In other words, Muybridge's motion photographs are sets of grids within grids – and indeed his entire ongoing exploration of the human figure and of animals in motion is a kind of grid, since Muybridge's approach remained the same, subject after subject. Of course, these grids prefigure the essential grid of the filmstrip.[8]

Regardless of how much Muybridge, or anyone else, actually studied the motion recorded in the motion photographs – his central compulsion seems to have been the recording of information rather than the detailed examination of it – his use of a consistently serial organization of both space and time found its way into the works of avant-garde filmmakers interested in studying film's historical origins and the fundamentals of its technology. The way was smoothed by the fact that during the mid–1960s many painters, sculptors, and musicians were exploring serial organizations of imagery as a means of avoiding conventional, traditionally hierarchical arrangements of material, space, and time. A good many filmmakers, including all those whose work is the focus of subsequent chapters, have used serial organizations as a means of revealing how things move. In some cases, this interest in serial organization has resulted in films made in conscious homage to Muybridge: Instances include Morgan Fisher's *Documentary Footage* (1968, discussed briefly in the Fisher chapter of Part 1), Robert Huot's *Turning Torso Drawdown* (1971), Hollis Frampton's *INGENIVM NOBIS IPSA PVELLA FECIT* (1975), and George Griffin's *Viewmaster* (1976). While none of the films discussed in detail in the following chapters is exactly an homage to Muybridge, each film is structured serially and can be understood as a "motion study." The particulars of the serial structuring, and the rigorousness (or compulsiveness) with which the various grids are developed, reflect the sensibilities of the filmmakers. Together, the fifteen films provide a grid against which viewers can study their experiences of conventional (and critical) films.

Whereas Muybridge's deepest concerns seem to have been scientific, the Lumière brothers' primary concern was economic: Their fascination with motion pictures was a function of their work as camera manufacturers. Ironically, avant-garde filmmakers found a way of ignoring this dimension of the Lumières, and the Lumière films came to stand for, and to inspire, a nonmaterialistic approach to filmmaking. When Jonas Mekas dedicated *Walden* "to Lumière," the dedication was a reference to the excitement Mekas assumed the Lumière brothers must have felt when they confronted the visual world, as if for the first time, with their Cinématographe, and to their apparently innocent openness to the everyday experiences around them. For Mekas, and for others rediscovering the Lumières, the most notable dimension of their films was the seeming simplicity of the subjects on which they trained their cameras (a train arriving at a station, workers leaving a factory, children playing, a mother and father feeding their baby) and of the means used to record these subjects: Each film was a single, continuous, extended shot, recorded by a stable, mounted camera. For the Lumières, their choice of subjects probably had mostly to do with their desire to demonstrate the breadth of capabilities they saw in the Cinématographe, to show off the new technology itself (by using it to record familiar realities, they could be sure that viewers would focus on the magic of their machine), and no doubt they assumed that their juxtaposition of film after film, each recording a different subject or kind of subject, would be exciting for viewers.

But for filmmakers rebelling against the decadence of the Hollywood industry and its contempt for everyday, personal reality, the Lumières' films were a breath of fresh air. Seen from a context created by the history and current practice of industry moviemaking, the Lumières' subjects seemed to subtly polemicize the beauties and pleasures of everyday life and a populist admiration for workingclass people. The consistent use of the single continuous shot seemed a form of filmic mediation that allowed for a different kind of motion study: a sustained examination and appreciation of subjects for their wholeness and/or their visual and conceptual subtlety. If Muybridge can be said to represent the analysis of reality so that it can be studied, the Lumières can be said to represent the synthesis of reality so that it can be comprehended.

For avant-garde filmmakers interested in "reinventing" cinema, the Lumières' single-shot approach seemed ideal, and the result was that, beginning in the mid–1960s, a variety of filmmakers made single-shot films, often extending the basic form so that the single shot lasted for more than ten minutes.[9] All the films I've discussed in detail in this volume either use long, continuous shots or employ closely related means for creating a similar effect. And in general, the goal of these extended shots is much the same: to focus attention – an almost meditative level of attention – on subject matter normally ignored or marginalized by mass-entertainment film, and,

From the Lumière brothers' *L'Arrivée du train en gare* (1895). Courtesy Museum of Modern Art Film Stills Archive.

by doing so, to reinvigorate our reverence for the visual world around us and develop our patience for experiencing it fully.

The remaining fifteen chapters in this book are arranged in a manner that reflects the dimensions of Muybridge and the Lumières central in the particular films discussed. Each chapter provides an "extended look" at a particular film made between 1966 and 1987, though all the chapters include information about the filmmakers' other work, especially about films that help to clarify the films discussed in detail (and about related work by others). Each discussion explores the potential of the particular film for critiquing dimensions of the commercial cinema. It will be obvious that the films can be approached from other theoretical directions and used in a variety of contexts (indeed some of the films have been widely discussed elsewhere). But my goal is to provide a way of seeing each film that not only makes what some have considered difficult work reasonably accessible, but offers a way of using the films that can energize viewers' experiences with cinema of all kinds.

While the individual chapters provide in-depth discussions of particular films, the overall organization of the chapters facilitates comparisons of

The landscape in Larry Gottheim's single-shot *Fog Line* (1970).

films and types of films. The fifteen chapters are divided into a grid made up of three relatively distinct sections, five chapters each. The films discussed in Part 1 – Yoko Ono's *No. 4 (Bottoms)* (1966), Michael Snow's *Wavelength* (1967), Ernie Gehr's *Serene Velocity* (1970), J. J. Murphy's *Print Generation* (1974), and Morgan Fisher's *Standard Gauge* (1985) – focus on aspects of equipment, material, and process that make all kinds of film imagery possible, including the dramatizations (and/or documentations) of characters so central in the conventional cinema. The films in Part 2 focus on aspects of the tradition of film as dramatic narrative. Hollis Frampton's *Zorns Lemma* (1970), Laura Mulvey and Peter Wollen's *Riddles of the Sphinx* (1977), James Benning's *American Dreams* (1984), Su Friedrich's *The Ties That Bind* (1984), and Yervant Gianikian and Angela Ricci Lucchi's *From the Pole to the Equator* (1987) critique the commercial cinema's narrow range of narrative procedures. Part 3 expands the focus beyond the issue of storytelling, to critique the convention that filmmaking is a national (and nationalistic) enterprise. Each of the five films discussed at length – Warren Sonbert's *The Carriage Trade* (1973), Godfrey Reggio's *Powaqqatsi* (1988), Trinh T. Minh-ha's *Naked Spaces—Living Is Round* (1985), Yvonne Rainer's *Journeys from Berlin/1971* (1979), and Peter Watkins's *The Journey* (1987) – demonstrates ways in which cinema can move beyond its territorial heritage.

Within each section, individual chapters are arranged so as to traverse a certain cinematic terrain and provide a sense of development. The overall direction of the first section is continued in subsequent sections. Further, particular chapters in particular positions within sections are meant to res-onate with the chapters in those positions in the other sections. In terms of the types of critique it uses, *No 4 (Bottoms)* "belongs" in Part 1, but it also has more in common with *Zorns Lemma* and *The Carriage Trade* than with other films in Parts 2 and 3. Similarly, *Standard Gauge* resonates not only with the other films discussed in Part 1, but with *From the Pole to the Equator* and *The Journey* from Parts 2 and 3.

Together, the in-depth analyses of particular films and the organization of these discussions into a grid provide the opportunity for an extended "motion study" of film viewership on a number of different levels. Most obviously, literal and figurative journeys by characters are the central focus of the particular films analyzed, and each character's journey engages view-ers in a different form of conceptual travel in the theater. These journeys grow increasingly extensive, from chapter to chapter, and part by part. In the first section, "From Stern to Stem," the journeys are, in a literal sense, quite short, though their implications are considerable. Chapter 1 discusses Yoko Ono's *No. 4 (Bottoms)*, where the camera rigorously frames on the buttocks of people filmed walking in place on a treadmill: *They* may not get anywhere on this "journey," but Ono's film offers the viewer extensive conceptual travel. In Part 2, "Psychic Excursions," the focus is on journeys of consciousness, though in all instances the psychic travel of filmmakers (and the "journey" of those who experience the films) is imaged and/or catalyzed by literal journeys. The focus of Part 3, "Premonitions of Global Cinema," is films in which filmmakers have used the camera as a vehicle for traveling *through* the political, linguistic, and conceptual boundaries that divide the world, and the editing process as a way of honoring the distinctions among various regions and peoples while demonstrating their interconnectedness.

Together, the various journeys depicted in the films offer the reader the opportunity of a metanarrative, a "critical voyage" with a route largely determined by the mass-entertainment film (and television) industry. We come to avant-garde film with our preconceptions already formed and with the habit of resisting any interruption of our cinematic pleasure. This book's grid of extended looks at ingenious critical films can function as a backdrop against which viewers can measure their journeys across the boundaries that separate them from unfamiliar cinematic terrains, toward a larger awareness of Cinema.

Although each of the films discussed in the following chapters is of considerable interest and of considerable potential use to those interested in engaging in an ongoing critique of mainstream film, I certainly am *not* arguing that these particular fifteen films are *the* "Best Films" of the past decades. They are simply fifteen of the best films I am aware of for invigorating a cinematic critique of commercial moviegoing expectations. I debated for months about which particular films to use, and some decisions were little more than arbitrary. In many cases, particular filmmakers might well have been represented by another of their films. For example, Michael Snow's ↔ (1969) could as easily have been the focus of Chapter 3 as *Wavelength;* and Warren Sonbert's *Friendly Witness* (1989) could replace *The Carriage Trade*. In some instances, even the choice of filmmaker was difficult. Larry Gottheim (*Horizons*, 1973) or Robert Huot (*Rolls: 1971*) might have opened Part 2, instead of Frampton; Jonas Mekas's *Reminiscences of a Journey to Lithuania* (1971) could have been used instead of Friedrich's *The Ties That Bind;* and Johan van der Keuken's *The Way South* (1981) would fit perfectly into Part 3. The single most difficult film *not* to include was Peter Kubelka's *Unsere Afrikareise* ("Our Trip to Africa," 1966) which could have ended Part 2 or begun Part 3.

In any case, my goal is not to canonize, or further canonize, fifteen particular films, or even the approach I use them to exemplify, but to instigate a much more extensive use of the remarkable body of alternative cinema represented by these films. As I write this introduction, the ongoing tradition of critical cinema remains one of film history's most underappreciated achievements and one of its most underutilized classroom resources.

NOTES

1. I use *avant-garde film* as a general term to designate the cinematic terrain that has, at various points in its history, been called "underground film," "The New American Cinema," "experimental film," "experimental/avant-garde film," and so on. This very proliferation of terms is evidence of the size and diversity of this particular area of film history, as well as of the ongoing debate about how to understand it. No one term seems entirely satisfactory – including *avant-garde film*. Avant-garde is not only a military reference (traditionally, avant-garde filmmakers have been antimilitaristic), it suggests that the films so designated lead the way for more conventional types of cinema, which is only true in a most limited sense. Some avant-garde films have made breakthroughs in form and content that have been exploited by commercial filmmakers, but in general avant-garde filmmaking has

been a derivation of the industry, a response to it in content and form. For all its problems, however, *avant-garde film* probably has the widest currency of all the designations and, in film studies, is generally understood to refer to an ongoing history that has been articulated in different ways in different places. Most of the other terms tend to refer to particular manifestations of this history. The terms "the first film Avant-Garde," "the first Avant-Garde," and even "the Avant-Garde" (in caps), generally refer specifically to the Western European avant-garde filmmakers of the 1920s.

2. William Alexander's *Film on the Left* (Princeton, NJ: Princeton University Press, 1981) details this school.

3. For an overview of the formative influence of the French *ciné-club* on the film society movement, see Chapter 3 of Richard Abel's *French Cinema: The First Wave, 1915–1929* (Princeton, NJ: Princeton University Press, 1984).

4. The history of Cinema 16 and Amos Vogel's approach to exhibition are discussed in Scott MacDonald, "Amos Vogel and Cinema 16," *Wide Angle,* vol. 9, no. 3 (1987), pp. 38–51.

5. (New York: Oxford University Press, 1974).

6. See J. Hoberman and Jonathan Rosenbaum, *Midnight Movies* (New York: Harper & Row, 1983). Unlike many forms of avant-garde film that are the products of individual filmmakers working alone, the trash films are often produced by groups of people working in a rough simulation of Hollywood collaborative methods.

7. William C. Wees discusses the issue of visual perception in the work of Brakhage and other filmmakers in *Light Moving in Time* (Berkeley, CA: University of California Press, 1992).

8. Some filmmakers – Paul Sharits is a well-known instance – have mounted strips of motion picture film side by side in a grid to create visually arresting gallery installations of grids within the larger grid.

9. There are dozens of examples. The earliest instances I know of are Bruce Baillie's *All My Life* (1966, although the camera here isn't stationary) and *Still Life* (1966); several films included in the 1966 *Fluxfilm Program* assembled by George Maciunas (see Chapter 2); and Robert Nelson's *The Awful Backlash* (1967). In my teaching, the most useful single-shot films have been Larry Gottheim's *Blues* (1969) and *Fog Line* (1970), and Robert Huot's *Snow* (1971). I discuss these and other single-shot films in "Putting All Your Eggs in One Basket," *Afterimage* (American), vol. 16, no. 8 (March 1989), pp. 10–16.

Part I
From Stern to Stem

The very idea of making or using a film as a means of exploring dimensions of the film apparatus is a confrontation of the conventional assumption, implicitly accepted by movie producers and moviegoers alike, that the cinema is a "neutral" technology to be enjoyed without question and without investigation, and that, therefore, any attempt to draw sustained attention to the means of production of the film image is unnecessary, pretentious, "boring." By conducting extended investigations of the camera and filmstrip, the filmmakers in this section defy this conventional assumption.

The particular critical journey that begins with people walking in place on a treadmill (in *No. 4 (Bottoms)*), and continues across the inside of a New York loft (in *Wavelength*) down an institutional hallway (in *Serene Velocity*), to a Bayonne, New Jersey, backyard and a Vermont village (in *Print Generation*), and to the surrounds of Hollywood (in *Standard Gauge*) allows for a reexamination of the delimited space of the film frame, of the potentials of camera, lens, and celluloid, and of the many refinements of the cinematic apparatus developed in Hollywood and reappropriated by critical filmmakers. Of course, if one understands the apparatus of cinema as a particular product, or set of interrelated products, of Western rationalism and industrialization, then the explorations conducted in the following five chapters can be recognized as attempts to rethink cinematically this history and to break out of the restrictive patterns it has created – or, to put it another way, as a microcosm of developments that are literalized by the more fully macrocosmic explorations conducted in the films in Parts 2 and 3. After all, in one sense, the humble "globes" catalogued in *No. 4 (Bottoms)* represent the human species as fully as the most extensive voyage around the world, and even the most fully international film cannot show us more than what is enclosed (or illuminated) by the frame.

17

I

Yoko Ono

No. 4 (Bottoms)

Some of the filmmakers discussed in this volume were avid moviegoers as children and adolescents; others were not. Their moviegoing histories and habits, however, have no particular bearing on their ability to construct films that function as critiques of conventional mass-market movie making. All that is really necessary for the production of a critical film is the decision by a filmmaker to make a film that, for those who see it in a movie theater (or on videotape), will have impact *because of its difference from what is usually seen.* The particular kinds of critique filmmakers decide to develop, however, are often determined by their experiences – or lack of them – at the movies. By the time Yoko Ono began to make contributions to American avant-garde film history, she had already established herself as an important New York artist and, like Michael Snow, the subject of the next chapter, she saw her filmmaking – at least at the outset – as simply another arena within which she could function as an artist. Nevertheless, the films she was to make between 1966 and 1971 offer a variety of critical alternatives to the mass-market conventional cinema she had seen even before leaving Japan, some of them quite conscious.[1]

Before she began making films, Ono studied poetry and music at Sarah Lawrence College, and in 1956 married Toshi Ichiyanagi, a young modernist composer. Her life with Ichiyanagi brought her into contact with John Cage and Merce Cunningham and these contacts paved the way for her involvement in Fluxus, an art movement with roots in Dada and Duchamp. Fluxus proposed new forms of audience/artist interaction that would sidestep the traditional focus on the artist's tour de force performance. By the early 1960s Ono was producing performances and objects. In *A Piece for Strawberries and Violins* (1961), Yvonne Rainer stood up and sat down in front of a table stacked with dishes; after ten minutes, she smashed the dishes.

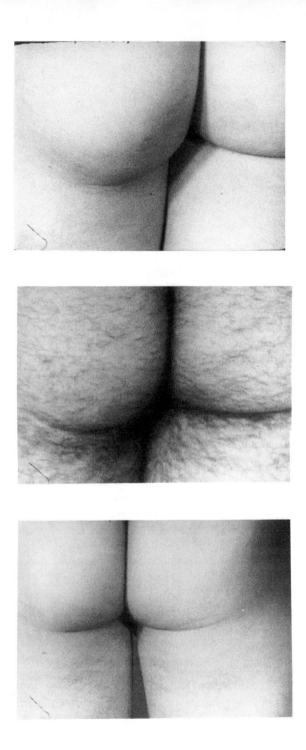

Rainer's actions were accompanied by "a rhythmic background of repeated syllables, a tape recording of moans and words spoken backwards, and an aria of high-pitched wails sung by Ono."[2] During *Cut Piece,* Ono sat quietly on stage while members of the audience came forward and cut off pieces of her clothing. Ono's objects also redefined the audience's relationship to art. *Painting to See the Room Through* (1961) was a canvas with a tiny hole in the center through which the viewer could "see the room." *Painting to Be Constructed in Your Head* (1962) asked viewers to examine three paintings and then combine them in their minds.

In 1964, Wunternaum Press published the first edition of *Grapefruit,* a compilation of written instructions for Ono projects.[3] *Grapefruit* remains the most extensive and useful compilation of Ono's "concept art," and it contains some of her earliest forays into cinema: Section 6, "Film," includes several proposals for films, in the form of mini film scripts. "Film Script 3," for example, is, "Ask audience to cut the part of the image on the screen that they don't like. Supply scissors." "Omnibus Film" directs a producer to

1. Give a print of the same film to many directors.
2. Ask each one to reedit the print without leaving out any of the material in such a way that it will be unnoticed that the print was reedited.
3. Show all the versions together omnibus style.

Later, Ono copyrighted other film scripts, including "Film No. 5 (Rape, or Chase)":

Rape with camera. 1 ½ hour colour synchronized sound.

A cameraman will chase a girl on a street with a camera persistently until he corners her in an alley, and, if possible, until she is in a falling position.

The camera will be taking a risk of offending the girl as the girl is somebody he picks up arbitrarily on the street, but there is a way to get around this.

Depending on the budget, the chase should be made with girls of different age, etc. May chase boys and men as well.

As the film progresses, and as it goes towards the end, the chase and the running should become slower and slower like in a dream, using a high-speed camera.

I have a cameraman who's prepared to do this successfully.[4]

Three bottoms from Yoko Ono's *No. 4 (Bottoms)* (1966).

Although most of Ono's film scripts have not become the basis for finished films, they do indicate a dimension of her film work that distinguishes it from the conventional cinema and from most avant-garde film as well. For Ono, the *concept* of a film is, essentially, the film; once the concept exists, anyone who wants to can produce a version of that concept. *Rape* (1969), *Fly* (1970), and *Up Your Legs Forever* (1970) were all based on mini-film scripts; but, from Ono's point of view, these particular versions of the concepts are no more definitive than any particular instance of a conventional film genre. Clearly, the Hollywood industry concept, male meets female and their relationship develops from hostility to love, or the concept, human takes actions that result in the creation of a monster that subsequently destroys its maker and terrorizes humankind, have produced dozens of specific instances no one of which is definitive. The same could be true of Ono's concept in "Film No. 5 (Rape, or Chase)." Not only does *Rape* depart in some ways from the original film script, Ono's instructions make clear that many different "camera rapes" are possible, either as subjects for individual films, or perhaps within a single film. Even as film scripts, in other words, Ono's concepts for films provide a critique of conventional cinema, by suggesting how narrow the traditional range of conceptual options for conventional films has been.

The first films Ono actually made had nothing to do with the film scripts. They were produced as part of a Fluxus film program organized by George Maciunas in 1966. Ono's contributions to the *Fluxfilm Program* included *Eyeblink* and *Match,* two single-shot films made with an especially high-speed camera, and *No. 4,* the first of two Ono films in which the subject is the human buttocks. *Eyeblink* and *Match* were instigated by Maciunas, who had invited several artists to come and use a camera that recorded imagery at 2,000 frames a second; all the filmmakers needed to do was decide on a subject: The resulting film would reveal the subject in such extreme slow motion that its original nature and impact would be entirely transformed. The three most interesting of the *Fluxfilm Program* single-shot films are Ono's *Eyeblink,* Joe Jones's *Smoke,* and Chieko Shiomi's *Disappearing Music for Face* in which Ono appears. For *Eyeblink,* Ono centered her own eye in the middle of the frame, then recorded a single blink. While the subject is obviously an eye, the framing and the camera speed combine to detach this eye from any conventional photographic or filmic context: The eye seems new and strange and its slow-motion blink causes it to seem momentarily sexually suggestive, evocative of other body parts (the effect is reminiscent of Willard Maas's 1943 *Geography of the Body,* in which various "nonerotic" areas of the body are filmed so that they evoke erogenous zones). Even Ono's focus on a blink is suggestive: A blink is an inevitable element of normal human vision; it's so fundamental, in fact, that we tend to forget it exists. To center even a short film on a blink is a way of responding to the conventional cinema's avoidance of everyday reality and its fetishization of the special moment, the tour de force performance of character and actor. Ironically, in *Eyeblink* viewers see an eye just at the fraction of a second when the eye itself is not seeing as a result of an automatic reflex that makes sight possible – or, to be more precise, is responding to what has just been imprinted on the retina, rather than taking in new stimulae.

The slow-motion films produced for *Fluxfilm Program* are reminiscent of both Muybridge and the Lumières. They suggest Muybridge since the slowing of the imagery facilitates "motion study" of the subjects recorded. They are reminiscent of the Lumières because they are one shot long, and because the subjects were chosen as a means of revealing the untapped potential of what was for Macuinas, Ono, and the others a new camera technology. The films function as critique, expecially because of their duration: They are not simply as long as they needed to be to get made, they are long as a means of undercutting audience expectations. And their slow pace implies that film history has room for more than a narrow range of cinematic pacing that is entirely a function of the conventions of narrative development. Nowhere is this more evident than in Shiomi's *Disappearing Music for Face* in which the change of Ono's expression from smile to no smile is so gradual that viewers never actually see Ono's mouth move; they only see that it *has moved.*

The other film Ono included in the *Fluxfilm Program* is No. 4, a 5½-minute silent film (the single shot films were all silent as well) during which the camera follows a series of naked buttocks walking. Each bottom is seen in a single, continuous shot; one shot follows another without interruption. The spatial and temporal grid set up by the consistent framing and the regular pace and order allows viewers to study and compare the motion of the buttocks. While there's no evidence that Ono had Muybridge in mind, her procedure (as well as the nakedness of her subjects) is similar enough to Muybridge's to have been an homage.

It was not until Ono moved to England that she was to have the resources necessary for producing extended film projects. But as soon as she was able to work more easily in film, she returned to the No. 4 concept. The feature film *No. 4 (Bottoms)* (80 minutes) was the result. The first idea Ono had for *No. 4 (Bottoms)* was visual. It developed out of her awareness of conventional movies: "originally I simply wanted to cover the screen with one

23

object, with something that was moving constantly. In the course of seeing films, I had never seen a film where an object was covering the screen all the way through.... The closest you get to what I mean is ... a cowboy or something standing with his back to the screen, but you always see a little background. The screen is never covered; so I thought, if you don't leave a background it might be like the whole screen is moving."[5] The original, Fluxus *No. 4* only approximated this visual concept, since the buttocks didn't quite fill the screen. For *No. 4 (Bottoms)*, Ono had a revolving treadmill built that allowed her subjects to walk in place, which in turn enabled the camera to record the walking buttocks so that they filled the screen consistently. The buttocks are framed so that the seams between the bottom of the buttocks and the top of the legs, and the crack between the cheeks of the buttocks, divide the frame into quarters. As the subjects walk, the screen is filled with motion.

While Ono's original concept may have been visual, however, her decision to focus the film on buttocks in particular makes the experience conceptual as well. In 1966 nudity on screen was rare in the conventional cinema; even the minimal nudity in Sidney Lumet's *The Pawnbroker* (1965) had caused controversy in the United States. For Ono to decide to devote a feature film to close-ups of buttocks was, on one level, a most obvious confrontation of conventional cinematic expectations. Of course, on another level, *No. 4 (Bottoms)* can be said to have extended the conventional: Audiences certainly attend films with the expectation of seeing exposed flesh. And yet even on this level, Ono undercuts standard expectations.

As was true in the original *No. 4*, Ono uses a grid organization made up of single-shot images of bottoms (each buttocks is on-screen for between ten and fifteen seconds) that makes comparisons of the bottoms easy. What is most clear as one bottom follows the next, especially given the ways in which we are trained to see bodies in the cinema and in the media in general, is that Ono included bottoms entirely without regard as to whether they would be considered attractive or acceptable. There are male and female buttocks, fat and lean bottoms, hairy and hairless, rounded and droopy bottoms, bottoms with and without imprints from underwear – bottoms of all kinds *except* the sorts of touched-up, carefully lit bottoms that fill fashion and girlie magazines, advertisements, and conventional films. Indeed, Ono's matter-of-fact acceptance of human bodies remains one of the liberating dimensions of *No. 4 (Bottoms)*; the film not only confronts expectations, it uses this confrontation to put us back in touch with reality.

The original *No. 4* had been silent. The feature version uses the soundtrack as a way of contextualizing the imagery. While she was filming the bottoms,

Ono was recording conversations with people involved in the project (those whose bottoms ended up in the film and those who refused to participate once they had realized the nature of the project) and the news coverage of the happening generated by the project. This sound material was edited so that, as we watch the grid of bottoms, we develop a sense of the process that produced the imagery we're looking at and its implications for Ono, for participants, and for the British media. Frequently, Ono and others discuss the "boredom" viewers of the finished film may be experiencing. In general, the soundtrack provides a bridge between the film's unconventional visual imagery and the audience. There are also particular intersections between the image and soundtrack. For example, as viewers see a bottom with a growth that makes this bottom particularly unattractive by conventional standards, Ono is heard talking about how "beautiful" bottoms are. Periodic "intersections" between image and sound reveal that Ono's editing was as carefully controlled as the filming of the bottoms.

The consistency of the overall organization of *No. 4 (Bottoms)* can cause viewers to become complacent and assume that there's nothing to see other than one bottom after another. But while the visuals continue in the same

From Ono's *Film No. 5 (Smile)* (1968).

graphic and temporal arrangement throughout the film, midway through the film's eighty minutes Ono begins to toy with the viewer's memory, by repeating some bottoms seen earlier, and passages of commentary heard earlier. Whereas the repeated sound bits are pretty obvious, the repeated bottoms are not – though from time to time a particular bottom reveals idiosyncrasies that identify it as a bottom seen before. Sometimes the visual and/or auditory context is different, sometimes it's the same. Once the film develops this mystery of whether a particular bottom has been seen before, the viewer's relationship with the bottoms becomes more personal: We look not to see a new bottom, but to see if we "know" a particular bottom already. The film's serial structure confirms this direction: Not only does Ono reveal more bottoms than most viewers have ever seen in eighty minutes (a way of demonstrating the esthetic/moral correctness of seeing bottoms in film), but her decision to use a temporal structure that allows her to avoid emphasizing or playing down any particular bottom suggests that while bottoms are endlessly distinctive, *worth looking at,* there's no point in exaggerating one bottom, or type of bottom, or the excitement that seeing bottoms ought to cause. *No. 4 (Bottoms)* is a comic film that allows us to laugh at the Big Deal made of human nudity and of the reproduction of the naked body in conventional film. Just as the people Ono filmed walked in place on the treadmill, getting nowhere in their "journey" except into a movie (and into a new way of thinking about film), her viewers' ultimate destination, at least conceptually, is a new look at those humble globes of muscle and fat that remain the literal foundation of the experience of cinema.

The next major film project Ono took on was also an extension of the earlier Fluxus films. In fact, the concept for *Film No. 5 (Smile)* (1968) was one of the first she had had when Maciunas asked her to come up with ideas; since Maciunas had promised Chieko Shiomi, who was in Japan at the time, that she could make a smile film, he dissuaded Ono from pursuing her interest – the compromise was that Ono would be in *Disappearing Music for Face.*[6] Later, when Ono realized that Shiomi's concept for a smile film was different from hers – "Chieko Shiomi's idea is beautiful; she catches the *disappearance* of a smile" – she felt free to pursue her own idea. *Film No. 5 (Smile)* is a fifty-one-minute sound film which records John Lennon's face at 333 frames per second, outdoors, in color, in long continuous shots. If *No. 4 (Bottoms)* is primarily an extension of Muybridge, *Film No. 5 (Smile)* is primarily an extension of the Lumières.

Early in the film, Lennon's face is largely immobile, blurring the distinction between a motion picture and still photograph. After a while, several tiny events occur: Lennon makes an "O" with his lips, an insect or a bird flies

26

across the image, and so on. Later on in the film, Lennon's face is more active: He blinks several times, sticks his tongue out, smiles broadly twice. The imagery is accompanied by sounds recorded outdoors at the time when Lennon's face was recorded. Ono offers viewers the opportunity to really *look* at a face, to study it: At times, it is as if Lennon's stream of consciousness is visible, passing across his countenance. *Film No. 5 (Smile)* creates a very unusual audience–film relationship. Those of us in the theater and Lennon seem to meditate on each other from opposite sides of the cinematic apparatus, joined together by Ono in a lovely, hypnotic stasis.

As the old saw goes, every journey begins with a single step. For Ono, and the other filmmakers discussed in Part 1, the first step was to revise our sense of what the film audience can be expected to look at. In *Eyeblink, Film No. 5 (Smile),* and especially *No. 4 (Bottoms),* subject matter that normally functions as means to an end in conventional cinema is extended and foregrounded (if the reader will forgive the pun, becomes an "end" in itself). The results may be frustrating for many viewers, but they demonstrate the potential for cinematic alternatives that are both thoughtful and revealing, and, for some, the source of new kinds of visual pleasure. The hundreds of men and women who agreed to appear in *No. 4 (Bottoms)* may have walked in place, but they continue to lead viewers in the direction of expanded options for cinema, and since the media has maintained its campaign of defining and relentlessly marketing a narrow range of "correct" human bodies, their endlessly varied bottoms – and Ono's cinematic commitment to them – continue to lead us back to reality.

NOTES

1. As an adolescent in Japan in the late 1940s, Yoko Ono was a regular moviegoer. She and her highschool classmates frequently sneaked into local movie houses, some to enjoy Doris Day and Rock Hudson and other American stars, others – the "intellectuals" – to see French films that had made their way to Japan. Ono was one of the "intellectuals"; she remembers Jean Cocteau's films in particular. See interview with Ono in Scott MacDonald, *A Critical Cinema* 2 (Berkeley, CA: University of California Press, 1992), p. 144.
2. Barbara Haskell, "Yoko Ono: Objects," *Yoko Ono: Objects/Films* (New York: Whitney Museum of American Art, 1989), p. 2.
3. *Grapefruit* has been republished in various forms in the years since – most recently in a Simon and Schuster Touchstone paperback edition in 1971.
4. Sixteen of the miniscripts were published in *Film Quarterly*, vol. 43, no. 1 (Fall 1989), pp. 16–21.
5. MacDonald, *A Critical Cinema* 2, p. 148.
6. MacDonald, *A Critical Cinema* 2, p. 146.

2
Michael Snow
Wavelength

Unlike Yoko Ono, Michael Snow has never been an avid moviegoer. He has always been more intrigued with music, painting, sculpture, and photography than with the conventional cinema. In fact, his decision to work with film was a function of his interest – an interest shared by many artists in the 1960s – in confronting the widespread cultural assumption (on the part of both "serious" artists and conventional community and commercial image makers) that a true artist was an expert in one particular arena of the fine arts, or at most, in a narrow range of related areas. For Snow and many other members of his generation, the artist was *precisely* the person who could make interesting works regardless of the medium or, more exactly, who saw the diversity of media as the central artistic challenge. Snow entered filmmaking not to respond to conventional filmmaking, but because film had come to be seen, within art circles, as a medium that expert *artists* tended to ignore. And yet, like Ono, Snow made films that remain very powerful critiques of conventional cinema and of the audience expectations it has engendered.

During the period before *Wavelength,* the film that established Snow's reputation as a filmmaker, he had served a self-imposed apprenticeship in two ways: He had made nonfilmic works that prefigured cinema, and he had produced three films. From 1961 until 1967 Snow explored what he called *The Walking Woman Works,* an extensive series of works in a very wide range of media in which the basic motif is a somewhat abstracted shape of a woman walking.[1] The Walking Woman pieces appeared both in and out of art galleries; silhouettes of the Walking Woman photographed on the street; she made a well-known appearance as a set of sculptures at Expo '67 in Montreal; paintings and collage works using her shape were exhibited in galleries; she was printed on T-shirts; and so on. While *The*

Walking Woman Works had at first nothing directly to do with film, the basic idea of using the same figure (a figure in motion) over and over, always in a changed context, has a good bit in common with the filmstrip. Snow's engagement with the serial form seems to have paved the way for his decision to make movies.

Also relevant are several photographic pieces in which Snow employed serial images.[2] In *Atlantic* (1966–7), thirty photographs of ocean waves are mounted in a grid (5 images high by 6 images across): Each image is separated from the others by tin sheets that divide the grid into thirty separate boxes. Other, later photographic works – *A Wooden Look* (1969), *Of a Ladder* (1971), *Glares,* (1973), and *Light Blues* (1974) – also use serial photographs, arranged in grids, though without the mediation of tin sheets. In Eadweard Muybridge's motion study photographs the function of the grid organization was ostensibly to allow viewers to study the particulars of the changes in the position of the subjects recorded by the camera. In Snow's serial grids, however, the photographic "subjects" are constants which allow us to focus on the effects and implications of the recording process and/or the elements involved in presenting the images. In *Glares,* eighty-one individual photographs of an empty grid lit by a lamp were taken from a camera mounted on a tripod, but readjusted so that each image centers a given rectangle in the grid; the eighty-one images were then mounted each in its corresponding grid position so that in the completed work viewers see the gap between the original grid and the photographic recording of it: they are primarily aware of the effects of the different levels of light on different sectors of the grid and of the "optical bend" that results from the camera's lens.

Snow's earliest films confirm his precinematic interests and reveal his increasing dexterity with the new medium. The most notable is *New York Eye and Ear Control* (1964), a thirty-four-minute sound film in which Snow's visual documentation of *The Walking Woman Works* is accompanied by a soundtrack of wildly free-form jazz, as a means of responding to the way in which music is used in conventional film, "especially the way music is subordinated to image. Even the greatest work of the greatest artist, J. S. Bach, is often used to set up a certain attitude in commercial films, and I've hated that for years. I wanted to do something where the music could *survive* and not only be a support for the image."[3] In *Wavelength* he used what he had learned in the early films to develop a fundamentally new form of cinematic critique.

While *Wavelength* was the most unusual film Snow had made, it was in keeping with his earlier work.[4] The appearance of images of the Walking

Woman in *Wavelength* and the film's use of one of the stills that had formed the photographic grid in *Atlantic* tied the new work to specific previous projects. For audiences who saw the finished film in the late 1960s, however, and for nearly all audiences who see it now, *Wavelength* is, quite simply, outrageous. The source of the outrage is the film's organization of action: the way it handles time, space, and imagery both on the screen and on the soundtrack. In his original description of *Wavelength* for the Fourth International Experimental Film Festival in Knokke-Le-Zoute, Belgium, in 1968 (the description has been regularly reprinted in the *Filmmakers' Cooperative Catalogue*), Snow called *Wavelength* "a continuous zoom which takes 45 minutes to go from its widest field to its smallest and final field." The soundtrack provides an analog to the visuals; a few moments after the film has begun, Snow introduces a sine wave that rises in pitch, shortening the wavelengths continually until the conclusion of the film. Other things are heard – just as things are seen, besides the effects of the zoom – but the sine wave dominates the auditory field the way the zoom structures the visuals. For nearly all viewers, the idea of structuring a film around a zoom across a New York loft and a rising sine wave is nearly untenable; such a principle could not be the foundation for a *real* movie. And yet, *Wavelength* is not only a movie, it is a movie about motion pictures, just as much late–1960s painting and sculpture was about painting and sculpture – particularly its material and conceptual foundations.

Snow's description of *Wavelength* would seem to locate the film not in the Muybridge tradition mentioned in connection with *The Walking Woman Works* and Snow's grid photographs, but in the "Lumière" tradition. Until the final minutes of the film, when the zoom closes in on the still image of waves from *Atlantic,* the viewer meditates on a limited expanse of real life: a loft space and those portions of Canal Street visible outside the loft windows (and sometimes in the reflections of windows across the street). While *Wavelength* is half the length of a conventional feature, its reconstruction of film action makes it seem to most viewers twice as long. Essentially, *Wavelength* demands extended patience for the act of being in a movie theater watching images. Snow assumes that viewers will not only watch what's on the screen and listen to the sound, but will watch themselves watching and listening. As in a good many of Snow's earlier sculptural pieces, the viewer's position as viewer is a central element – an idea Snow often explores in later films, including the more recent *Seated Figures* (1988)

Empty loft; man (Hollis Frampton) falling dead; woman (Amy Taubin) discovering the dead body, from Michael Snow's *Wavelength* (1967).

31

in which, so far as I can tell, the title refers literally, and exclusively, to the audience.

While the avant-garde tendency to extend the Lumière single-shot film is evident in *Wavelength*, Snow's film is far from a single shot and, in fact, his zoom is not "continuous" in the sense that his description seems to suggest. Snow's original description of the film was implicitly predicated on the assumption that the zoom would *seem* continuous to people who had never seen a film structured around an extended zoom. While the zoom in *Wavelength* is generally regular, it is – to current eyes – less continuous than periodic: During the majority of the film, the zoom lens is adjusted, in small increments, with extended pauses between the increments. Near the conclusion of *Wavelength*, the zooming becomes more frequent – almost continuous, in fact – then stops entirely for the final minutes of the film. The periodic quality of the zoom aligns the film with the Muybridge serial tradition: The space of the loft is an implicit grid (the windows, ceiling, walls divide the visual field into squares and rectangles), and the regular pauses and adjustments of the lens divide the zoom's focal length, and the film's duration, into a space/time grid, with which we can measure and compare a wide range of ways in which a filmmaker can distort, or recreate, the imagery the camera records. While this description may recall the minimalist esthetic of the 1960s, *Wavelength* is far from a minimal work. Much of what we expect from commercial movies is eliminated, but Snow replaces it with a wealth of visual and auditory information, including a variety of references to conventional cinema.

Wavelength opens with what appears to be a narrative (or a set of actions being documented): Two women carry a bookcase into the loft space and leave. Snow begins by invoking the convention, however, only to undercut it: A moment of color flickers and the first of the zoom movements interrupts the development of this opening action, which continues as the women reenter and apparently turn on the radio ("Strawberry Fields Forever" plays in toto) before leaving again. Nothing further happens on the film's narrative level for another ten minutes or so, when we hear the noise of smashing glass: A man (Hollis Frampton) staggers into the room and falls unconscious. Near the end of the film, one of the women (Amy Taubin) reenters the apartment, discovers the body, phones someone named Richard, tells him she thinks the man is dead, and asks him to come over. He apparently agrees, and she leaves the loft to meet him. At the very end of the film sirens are heard, presumably indicating that the police or an ambulance have arrived.

The narrative in *Wavelength* is at best skeletal; it accounts for only a small portion of screen time. But it is one of the film's most potent critical gestures. Avid filmgoer or not, Snow was aware that when a filmmaker begins a film with narrative action, viewers will assume the film is *about* that action. And he was certainly aware that a sudden, mysterious death is the sort of action one can expect in conventional films. As a result, his decision to invoke characters and plot, and then to ignore them for most of the film (in fact, to ignore them until viewers have given up their expectations, and then reinvoke them, only to ignore them again) is a way of challenging convention. Indeed, this particular way of using narrative is reminiscent of a similar challenge to conventional literary narrative by Alain Robbe-Grillet and the *Nouveau Roman* movement, which has had a direct impact on film history in such films as *Last Year at Marienbad* (1961, directed by Alain Resnais, scenario by Robbe-Grillet).

Throughout his career, Snow has punctuated his work in film and in other media with humor, some of it subtle, wry, some of it obvious, corny. For many viewers *Wavelength* is certainly not funny; moviegoers expect pleasure of particular kinds, and when a filmmaker refuses to deliver this pleasure, many viewers become quite hostile. Nevertheless, for Snow the refusal to provide what he knows most viewers expect is something of a prank. Nowhere is this more evident than after the man staggers into the loft and dies. Dramatic action, and especially violent action, is so often the focus of the camera – often we see it in close-up, in slow motion, and repeatedly – that Snow's refusal to allow his camera to deviate from its consistent trajectory toward the loft's far wall is, for those who can put aside their frustration, an amusing manifesto: for Snow, action is clearly neither the focus nor the goal of filmmaking; yes, it certainly exists; it is certainly *one* resource a filmmaker can choose to use, but for a film artist its demands are not central. In *Wavelength* Snow marginalizes what conventional cinema fetishizes, and focuses on cinematic elements that in mass-market movies are at most decorative. He exploits "plot" primarily in the geometric sense.

Wavelength explores three particular elements in some depth: the effects of the zoom lens on the camera's representation of space; the effects of lighting, filmstock, filters, and related variables on the reproduction of imagery; and the nature and impact of film sound. The impact of the periodic zooming on the viewer's apprehension of the loft and the space visible outside the loft windows is central to the experience of *Wavelength*. The first sense of the loft is of deep space. By the end of forty-five minutes, the camera has zoomed in on a single small photograph on the far wall, which at the opening of the film is not even recognizable as a photograph. The zoom lens readjusts the camera's imaging of this space again and again, so that, gradually, it seems transformed from three dimensions to two, and so that the overall composition is continually redesigned. At first the loft windows are at the end of the "tunnel" of the loft; later they fill the screen; still later two windows frame a space on which the images of the Walking Woman and the photograph of the waves are mounted, and at the end the windows are no longer visible and the center space has become a flat background for the photograph, which gradually fills the screen. The reconstruction of the loft space by the zoom lens usurps the usual filmic narrative focus on the development of characters and their relationships. The potential of a particular lens to re-form what the camera and film record replaces the range of moral choices faced by conventional film characters.

As the zoom lens carries the viewer along its central axis toward the photograph of waves, Snow is continually altering the look of what is seen by filming at various times of day or night, with various kinds and levels of natural and artificial light, by using a variety of shooting and printing stocks, and by shooting through color transparencies. The result is a far wider range of colors and textures than any conventional film employs. In fact, the film's infrequent moments of consistent, uninterrupted naturalistic color function as a periodic reminder of the conventions Snow refuses to be limited by. At times Snow's interference with the photographic record of the loft makes for gorgeous imagery – breathtaking oranges and reds, yellows, and pinks; at other times the look of the same space changes so completely from one moment to the next that it's difficult to believe we're looking at the same room. In some instances we are oblivious to anything except the inside of the loft, at others our eye is drawn out the windows. At times we wait for further changes in the imagery, at other times we are bombarded by the strobe effect of continual changes. Snow intersperses these myriad variations during the forty-five minutes of *Wavelength* so that we are never sure what exactly we'll see next, or to put it in film-critical terms, so that the complacency created by conventional filmgoing, where the particulars of rhythm are relatively predictable, is continually confronted.

Snow's use of sound in *Wavelength* is a critical alternative to the sound in conventional movies. During the film's opening moments when the two women talk, viewers may assume that synchronized sound will be the rule in *Wavelength,* as it is in mass entertainment films. By the end of a few minutes, however, when the women enter the image for the second time, it is clear that Snow is beginning to undercut conventional sound expectations: The sound of the women's footsteps is clearly not synchronized. And even if viewers assume that "Strawberry Fields Forever" is playing on the radio they can see on the far side of the loft, the quality of the song and the fact that it doesn't seem to relate to any further narrative action (the lyrics do contain a pun on the experience of seeing *Wavelength:* "Living is easy with eyes closed...") undercut whatever expectations its original inclusion creates.

The film's most radical deviation from conventional sound expectations, however, is the sine wave that begins once "Strawberry Fields Forever" ends. This continuous sound is as different from standard film sound as Snow's decision to center on a zoom as a structural device is different from conventional plot. And the longer the sound is maintained, and the higher and more penetrating it gets, the more outrageous it seems: Many viewers react as if the sound assaults them, which it *does* periodically, as fully as the moments of flicker assault the eye. The sine wave is more than unconventional, however: It provides another Snow joke on the usual design of cinema soundtracks. If the shards of narrative included in *Wavelength* suggest a suspense thriller or *cinéma noir,* the slow, relentless rise of the sine wave's pitch suggests the curve of rising tension so common to these genres. Of course, the joke is that *here,* the rising tension is not a function of the characters' actions, but of *Wavelength*'s "attack" on the audience. Such implications are reconfirmed at the end when the siren seems to descend

The final image of *Wavelength.*

35

out of the sine wave: Help has arrived not only for Amy, but for the exhausted viewer.

The final irony in *Wavelength*, figuratively and literally, is the fact that the long journey across the loft and through the catalogue of visual options Snow explores, and the accompanying auditory curve of rising tension, deliver the audience to the absolute nemesis of the conventional cinema: to a still photograph viewed in silence for several minutes; instead of moving forward, *Wavelength* seems to return us to the pre-cinema – and yet we realize that the drama of Snow's coda is not only a final element in his undercutting of conventional movie history and current practice, but that the particulars of the photograph on which we meditate in silence refer to the experience we've just completed: The ocean waves in the image are a metaphor for both the periodic motions of the zoom lens and for the oscillations of the sine wave; they may also suggest the "ocean" of visual possibilities the conventional cinema refuses to traverse.

NOTES

1. From November 1983 until January 1985, a retrospective of Snow's Walking Woman Works toured Canada and the United States. An extensively illustrated, well-documented catalogue, *Walking Woman Works: Michael Snow 1961–67*, was published in connection with the touring show, by the Agnes Etherington Art Centre, Queen's University, in Kingston, Ontario.

2. Regina Cornwell discusses Snow's photographic work in Chapter 3 ("Photographic Objects") of *Snow Seen: The Films and Photographs of Michael Snow* (Toronto: Peter Martin, 1980). See also Amy Taubin, "Doubled Visions," *October*, no. 4 (Fall 1977), pp. 33–42.

3. From an interview with Snow in Scott MacDonald, *A Critical Cinema 2* (Berkeley, CA: University of California Press, 1992), p. 60.

4. *Wavelength* is the most discussed of Snow's films, and one of the most consistently discussed of all critical films. The two most extensive, and most extensively documented, discussions of the film are those in Cornwell's *Snow Seen* (Chapter 4, pp. 60–79) and in R. Bruce Elder's *Image and Idea: Reflections on Canadian Film and Culture* (Waterloo, Ontario: Wilfred Laurier University Press, 1989), pp. 188–213.

3
Ernie Gehr
Serene Velocity

For Ernie Gehr, as well as for Ono and Snow, making movies is a way of creating experiences that are so different from conventional movie experiences that they become critiques of the conventions. But while Ono and Snow are *artists* who have used the motion picture camera to broaden their repertoire and to expand their audience, Ernie Gehr is more precisely a *film artist*. While Ono and Snow are generalists, Gehr is a specialist. By the late 1960s, film's increasing prestige as a medium with which fine art experiences could be created had led some filmmakers to an interest in the intrinsic qualities of this particular medium. Just as many 1960s painters and sculptors were concerned with exposing the "essential," theoretically irreducible conditions of the experience of painting and sculpture, filmmakers began to attempt a "metaphysics" of the cinematic apparatus. Ernie Gehr was in the vanguard of this project. Each Gehr film is a voyage into the particular conditions of the film's production and a discovery of the immense untapped visual and conceptual potential of these conditions. The results dramatically demonstrate the narrow parameters of conventional moviemaking. Although the scope of this discussion does not allow for a review of all Gehr's films, *Serene Velocity* is best understood as one of several cinematic investigations of three elements of the motion picture camera: the camera obscura, the lens, and the filmstrip.

Gehr has always been unusually reticent about his life, and as a result we don't know a good deal about how he came to make the earliest of his films currently in distribution; but, by the time he made *Morning* (1968), he was clearly a sophisticated filmmaker, capable of using the film experience as a means of exposing and considering specific elements of the mechanical/chemical apparatus of cinema. *Morning* is a brief (4½-minute) visual interpretation of a portion of Gehr's apartment at dawn: The end of a bed and

the legs of someone presumably still sleeping and a cat are visible – but the personal elements are basically a context for the film's focus on light. The camera points toward a window that opens onto an alley; by working with the single-framing function of the camera and the aperture, Gehr takes control of the light this window lets into the space: We can see – or seem to see – its actual substance.

Of course, the moment we consider what is actually occurring, as the light seems to flood the space one moment and to reveal it in an ordinary way a fraction of a second later, we realize that the actual "room" into which the light flows is not the apartment, but the camera box. Gehr reminds us that the movie camera is, essentially, a "room" into which light is admitted through the "window" of the aperture. This is more than metaphor; it is a witty encapsulation of the history of a crucial element of the cinematic apparatus. Still and motion picture cameras developed as miniaturizations of the cubical rooms Western people have traditionally built as living spaces. In fact, the original camera obscuras were rooms in which the influx of light was more intensively controlled than the light through the windows of normal rooms. *Morning* reveals a conventional room space *and* the technological intensification of it which ultimately made still and motion pictures possible. A second dimension of Gehr's evocation of the evolution of cinema becomes evident if one notices that the powerful flickering of the light flooding through the apartment window is reminiscent of the experience of looking directly at a movie projector while it's running. In a general sense, the rooms we live in are theaterlike, as well as cameralike. Each morning, the light of the sun projects into our living space, revealing our physical surround. The movie projector is merely one important development among many in the long history of the technological domestication of lighting. As we sit in a theater watching *Morning*, we are face to face with the two historical processes – the development of the camera and of the projector – which came together at the dawn of cinema history in the Cinématographe.

In the years since *Morning*, Gehr has completed a series of distinguished films, each of which throws the extreme conventionality of industry cinema – and its continual pretension of newness – into relief. More than any other film, however, *Serene Velocity* established Gehr's reputation, and, despite the remarkable films he's made since 1970 – *Eureka* (1974–9) and *Table* (1976) most notably, perhaps – it remains his best known film, and for good reason: *Serene Velocity* creates an experience that is rigorously simple

Three consecutive frames from Ernie Gehr's *Serene Velocity* (1970).

(even minimal), but visually fascinating and conceptually fertile. The film's simple structure combines elements of Muybridge and the Lumières in much the same way *Wavelength* does. Basically, all the viewer sees, for twenty-three minutes, is a single, bare, institutional hallway (specifically, a hallway in a classroom building at the State University of New York at Binghamton, where Gehr taught for a time), filmed by a stationary camera. While the view of the hallway is continuous, however, it is far from uninterrupted. When *Serene Velocity* was first shown to audiences, viewers were often puzzled about how Gehr had produced the film's pulsating, superactive image. In fact, the means were not complicated, though it took a filmmaker entirely free of preconceptions about how movies are made to think of them. Having positioned his camera to look down the hallway, Gehr filmed the space four frames at a time, beginning midway along the focal range of his zoom lens and adjusting the zoom first in one direction, then in the opposite direction from the lens's midpoint, in equal and progressive alternating increments, until he had filmed the space from virtually every position between the midpoint and the two ends of the lens's focal range. The resulting film is serial, gridlike, both graphically (the hallway is all squares and rectangles within squares) and temporally (the film maintains its pulsating four-frame beat throughout); it allows the viewer to study the way in which Gehr's procedure transforms the space and the viewer's experience.

For many first-time viewers *Serene Velocity* is infuriating. Given their conventional training, they have no idea of what they are supposed to be seeing, other than a relentlessly repeated shift between two versions of the same space. On the other hand, if they can allow themselves to actually *look* at the film (certainly one of the first tendencies in many viewers, when confronted with powerfully critical films, is to shut down the eyes and/or mind: One can "watch" the films without seeing them), a set of developments in the seemingly unchanging image become apparent. As the zoom lens gradually moves us back and forth along the hall, the doors, ashtrays, and other details of the hallway move in and out of the image: At one focal length we may see a certain door; a few moments later and a few increments further along the focal range of the lens, the door has disappeared. While all changes in the hallway are created by the rigorous procedure Gehr devised for the camera, near the conclusion of the film we can see, from the light in the glass of the doors at the far end of the hallway, that it's dawn.

As in *Morning*, the "subject" of *Serene Velocity* can be seen as a metaphor (and more than a metaphor) for the particular element of film technology that allows the "subject" to be recorded in precisely the way we see it: The hallway is to the building what the lens is to the camera; both are long, narrow spaces that provide access to other spaces. Or, to put it another way, the zoom lens is the "hallway" through which light travels from outside the camera into the photosensitive darkness. If the camera box is a miniaturization and intensification of the rooms in which we live, lenses are miniaturization and intensifications of the spaces by means of which these rooms are accessed. Even the fact that the window at the end of the hallway becomes light at dawn might work within this parallel: In many movie cameras the end of a roll of film is signaled by a light one sees in the viewfinder.

Serene Velocity does more than develop an ingenious parallel between its ostensible visual subject and the particular means by which this subject is revealed. The silent evolution of the imagery of the hallway makes available a wide range of different film experiences, some of them, paradoxically, the opposite of others. In fact, the film's journey through the hallway/lens is an axis along which these other experiences are ranged. Of course, to a degree, what anyone sees during a screening of *Serene Velocity* depends on that individual's personal state of mind, and yet I would guess that any reasonably attentive viewer who watches the entire film will discover several different experiences. Perhaps the most obvious has already been mentioned – the feeling of being thrown relentlessly backward and forward four times each second (the lens was readjusted every four frames; the film is screened at sixteen frames per second). Since Gehr was moving incrementally away from the midpoint of the zoom lens focal range toward the extremes at either end, the perceptual gap between successive four-frame units of the film grows continually greater for twenty-three minutes. Of course, most of us do not maintain our attention on *Serene Velocity* at a single, unvarying level. Indeed, as violent as the successive changes in image can feel, they can be instantly transformed by the eye/mind into a very different visual experience. If one does not attempt to see the successive images of the hallway as individual three-dimensional spaces revealed in Renaissance perspective, if one doesn't rigorously focus in on the successive images, *Serene Velocity* can seem to be a flat, graphically distinct, nearly abstract image which regularly flashes between two states, like a neon sign. In fact, if the viewer sees the image as the two-dimensional space it really is, rather than as the three-dimensional space of which it is an illusion, the film can seem quite meditative: The square-within-square organization created by the lines of the doorways and light fixtures is reminiscent of classic mandalas. In other words, the film is simultaneously violent and meditative, depending on the nature of the visual experience the viewer decides to participate in at any given moment.[1]

Once it is evident that *Serene Velocity* is proceeding in a specific, predictable direction at a uniform rate, and that there is no one correct way of looking at the film, some viewers experiment with the specifics of their own apprehension of the imagery: At some point during my second viewing, I began blinking my eyes so as to try to see only one set of images of the hall, or to focus on a specific detail visible in only one set of the alternating images. Of course, the very opportunity for the viewer to choose how to see a particular film is itself an implicit critique of the assumption of commercial filmgoing, that each specific movie should be apprehended in one particular way and that within the film each individual cinematic moment has a precise function in ensuring that this one form of apprehension occurs. Viewers may refuse to participate in the particular series of emotions a director may try to orchestrate, but, if they do, they are aware that they are "reading" the film "against the grain."

The fact that Gehr is able to energize one of the dullest contemporary spaces (what is duller than an institutional hallway?) into a complex visual/conceptual experience is more than a tribute to his imagination; it dramatizes his esthetic position. For Gehr, the magic of the movie camera is its ability to free us from visual habits, especially those we've developed at the movie theater. The industrial history of film has impoverished our sight by endlessly reconfirming a narrow range of in-theater experiences, in which each narrative moment is a means for delivering us to the film's conclusion; in *Serene Velocity,* Gehr transforms a space designed for the purpose of delivering students to the rooms where they have educational business (a space which in a conventional film would have much the same function vis-à-vis the characters) into a highly energized, multifaceted visual experience.

If none of the films Gehr has completed since *Serene Velocity* has achieved that film's reputation, several are of equal interest and all are worth seeing: a new Gehr film remains something of an event. *Morning* can be said to encapsulate elements of the prehistory of cinema; *Eureka,* which Gehr worked on from 1974 through 1979 (sometimes under the title *Geography*) – deals ingeniously with the medium's subsequent history. To make *Eureka,* Gehr used a brief film made between 1903 and 1905, presumably to be shown on the front of a Hale's Tours coach: the camera is mounted on the front of a trolley and records the trolley's journey from the moment it turns onto Market Street in San Francisco until it reaches the Ferry Building and the end of the line (where a wagon with "Eureka, California" printed on the side crosses the image).[2] By rephotographing the original single-shot film a frame at a time, Gehr stretched the original trolley ride and allows us access to at least two levels of cinema history. On one hand, we confront the social history of the early twentieth century, within which the history of cinema was beginning (the date on the Ferry Building – 1896 – is suggestive in a film-historical context). The original film must have emphasized the excitement of a fast-moving trolley ride down Market Street; Gehr's slowed-down version retains the exciting moments (people move across the tracks so close to the front of the trolley that we can't imagine they won't be injured), but allows us to examine the environment of the street and the ways in which the people who saw the camera responded to it. Market Street circa 1903 seems to have been a model of functional anarchy: The roadway is crowded with all manner of vehicles and pedestrians, all of them vying for space, True, the vehicles on the right side of the road generally move in one direction; those on the left, the opposite way; but, beyond this, it seems a case of every vehicle for itself. The energy of the street, the collision of the many different worlds represented by the varied vehicles, and the pleasure people take in performing for the camera make *Eureka* a period piece with as much resonance as the most elaborate contemporary recreations of that era – Coppola's Lower East Side in *The Godfather 2* (1974), for example.

Market Street in San Francisco circa 1903, from Gehr's *Eureka* (1979).

But while *Eureka* allows us to experience San Francisco at the beginning of the century – watching the film is reminiscent of rides at Disney World and Epcot Center – Gehr's painstaking re-presentation of the original footage reveals a different form of history. In the years since the original film was shown, the prints that remain have decayed, so that the contemporary viewer must experience the original imagery through a curtain of scratches and other forms of decomposition. The journey down the trolley tracks in *Eureka* is also a trip through the time that has intervened between then and now, as that time is represented indexically on the filmstrip. The fact that the original film was recorded from the front of a trolley makes this other historical process particularly suggestive, since the essential mechanical technologies at work in trolleys and in cinema – and their shared limitation: friction – are historically related.

Of course, although *Eureka* is an elegy to a lost age and a decaying technology, it also reconfirms the remarkable power of cinema. As a result of the combination of the technologies explored in *Morning, Serene Velocity,* and *Eureka* (and Gehr's other films), we can still see these people; they are alive as we watch. As we travel along the filmstrip and along the "strip" that was Market Street, they gaze at us and we at them through time and space, by means of a "corridor" that simultaneously allows them access to the "dark room" of our consciousness and gives us access to the world in which they lived and moved. Gehr demonstrates that the cinematic apparatus is, like us, part material and part something more.

NOTES

1. Another experience is suggested by the joke Ken Jacobs made about *Serene Velocity* when he introduced the film at SUNY–Binghamton the first time I saw it: Jacobs said he found it a *sexy* film. Of course, on one level nothing could be less sexy than an institutional hallway, and yet, if one focuses on the red "EXIT" sign above the doorway that bisects the hallway, especially near the end of the film when the gap between the successive images is particularly dramatic, the exit sign seems to thrust forward toward us, as though it were a phallus.
2. For information on Hale's Tours see Raymond Fielding, "Hale's Tours: Ultra-realism in the Pre-1910 Motion Picture," in John L. Fell, *Film before Griffith* (Berkeley, CA: University of California Press, 1983), pp. 116–30.

4
J. J. Murphy
Print Generation

J. J. Murphy became seriously interested in film in the late 1960s as a student at the University of Scranton. Like many filmgoers of his generation, he was drawn to those foreign feature films which seemed so different from Hollywood movies, and, more fully than most of his contemporaries, he became deeply involved in what was then called "Underground Film," attending screenings regularly in New York City and making alternative cinema available in Scranton. Subsequently, he became committed to filmmaking as a means of critiquing the conventional film experience. From the beginning, Murphy's interest was less in the fundamental elements of the film apparatus that fascinated Gehr than in the transformative power of the camera and projector and their potential as experimental tools. While Gehr develops a filmic version of the formalism in the fine arts so pervasive during the 1960s, Murphy's films are more fully instances of the Process Art that fascinated artists in a variety of fields during the 1970s.

Three of Murphy's first four films are one shot long. *Highway Landscape* (1972) is a 6½-minute, ground-level meditation on a space of rural Iowa highway (with the carcass of a dead animal in the lower right quadrant of the image and a tree in the background). From time to time, the approach of a vehicle is dramatically presaged by the soundtrack, though, since the sound is monaural, we are never sure from which direction the vehicle will flash through the frame. The unusual gaze of the camera in *Highway Landscape* was a conscious declaration of cinematic principle, Murphy's way of demonstrating his determination to develop new ways of seeing. *In Progress*, also made in 1972 (with Murphy's teacher Ed Small), combines the experience of extended meditation on a single image with a temporal grid that enables us to study the process of change – the visual *motion* – in a lovely rural Iowa landscape: Murphy (and sometimes others, at his direction)

45

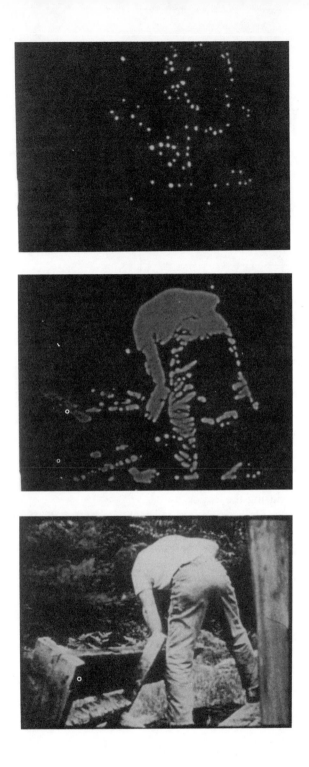

filmed the scene for a few seconds once a day, from the late summer of one year to the early summer of the next; when the shooting was done, the film was essentially finished. *In Progress* is a beautiful film, and a fascinating and vivid demonstration of how external conditions of light determine the nature of a camera's "reproduction" of a scene. *In Progress* provides a transition from the more Lumièresque quality of Murphy's first three films, to the more Muybridgian quality of his first longer film: *Print Generation* (1974, 50 minutes).

Print Generation uses a serial structure as regular and relentless as the structure of *Serene Velocity,* in order to examine conditions of viewership, not only in the general sense that all critical films examine conditions of viewership (by posing cinematic alternatives to conventional audience expectations that recontextualize and redefine these expectations), but specifically as the viewing experience is determined by the material nature of color film. Of course, it is nearly an axiom of mass-entertainment film that the viewer normally be as little conscious as possible of the material conditions, and limitations, of the medium. When scratches are visible in a print of a movie, the audience can be expected to abide by the unspoken convention of ignoring these distractions as fully as possible, to pretend in fact that the scratches are not there. For avant-garde filmmakers engaged in a critique of cinematic conditions and conditioning, however, such elements are possible subjects, as has already been suggested in connection with Gehr's *Eureka. Print Generation* provides an extended exploration of the fragility of the filmstrip and its inevitable entropy over time: particularly the loss of photographic quality, and of color quality especially, in the process of making prints.[1]

Like most of those who study film, Murphy had learned that a print of a photograph or a motion picture is never equal, in terms of photographic quality, to the original, and that further, a *print* of a *print,* a second-generation print, will inevitably provide less perfect detail than a print made from the original. As a filmmaker exploring cinematic basics, Murphy was particularly concerned with this process, in at least two ways. First, he experienced, and watched other filmmakers experience, the trauma of having a laboratory make a print of a film and discovering that the result was significantly different from the original. Second, as a student of film history, Murphy recognized that audiences of conventional movies and alternative films alike do not always see first-generation prints of the movies they watch.

Three stages of one of the images (Norman Bloom sawing wood) from J. J. Murphy's *Print Generation* (1974).

In fact, if one teaches classic film history, the question of print quality — and the more basic fact that when classic 35mm films are studied in institutions of higher learning, they are generally studied as 16mm prints — is often an important issue. If imagery is information, the decay of imagery (even if it's an inevitable part of the existence of this imagery) is the destruction of information. Murphy decided to explore the implications of this issue with rigor and in detail.

He decided to make a film and then submit it to an experimental printing process that would involve the laboratory making a contact print of his original, then a contact print of that print, then a contact print of *that* print, and so on, not only until the imagery revealed a noticeable gap between original and x-generation print, but until the imagery had decayed so entirely that a viewer would have no way of identifying the original images.[2] Murphy recognized that, laboratory costs being what they are, he would need to work with a short film since he would be making dozens of prints of prints. And he realized that, if the resulting process were going to reveal sufficient information, the brief film would need to include varied imagery. He finally settled on a one-minute diary loop that included sixty discrete one-second images (the function of the images being diaristic, instead of conventionally spectacular, was to ensure that the process of printing and reprinting — rather than any pyrotechnics in the original imagery — would be the viewer's focus, a choice reminiscent of the Lumières' use of everyday images in their earliest films to ensure that the magic of the Cinématographe would be the viewer's central focus). Murphy hired a laboratory to make print generations of the loop until all photographic quality had disappeared, until all or nearly all of the emulsion had been removed by successive generations of printing.

Once he received the fifty print generations back from the laboratory, Murphy edited them together in a manner determined in part by his process. Since he had used the *contact* printing process (where raw printing stock is laid face to face against an original or a print, and exposed to the light, producing a mirror image of what is printed), Murphy ended up with twenty-five generations of the imagery in one configuration, and twenty-five with the imagery in the opposite configuration. He decided to flip the one set so that viewers would always see the imagery in the same configuration, though this meant that the flipped generations would be in a slightly different focal range than the others, due to the thickness of the celluloid itself. The finished film first shows "A Wind," the first, third, fifth, seventh,... generations, then "B Wind," the second, fourth, sixth,... generations. "A Wind" presents the loop in its most degenerate form, then moves, print by print, to the first-generation print of the loop. After the "A Wind" title, and a re-focusing of the projector, "B Wind" presents the second-generation print, then moves back – print by print – to the imagery in its most degenerated form. Murphy decided on a soundtrack that would be a reverse analog to the visuals: he recorded one minute of ocean sounds on a tape recorder, then recorded that recording with a second recorder, and so on, for fifty generations. The ocean sounds grow distorted and then unrecognizable. As we watch "A Wind" we see twenty-five generations of the ocean sounds as they disintegrate; as the images "decay" during "B Wind," the ocean sounds are reconstituted.

Print Generation directs viewers toward two general aspects of the world beyond the film frame that condition our understanding of what we see inside the frame: the material nature and history of the printed film image itself and the cultural/psychological surround within which the audience sees and interprets the imagery. The viewer's experience of *Print Generation*, especially during the first half, tends to be puzzling (until it's clear that the same limited number of images is being seen in the same order, again and again), then rather dramatic: Once viewers are aware that there are sixty separate images, they inevitably attempt to predict what the images will look like once they're "completed." In almost all cases, these predictions undergo an evolutionary process that is dependent on the particular nature of the "stratas" of film emulsion revealed in given prints and on the par-ticular state of the soundtrack. While the process documented in *Print Generation* is about as different as can be from the narrative development of a conventional movie, the film's first half does engage viewers in an experience analogous to a suspense thriller. Each generation of images pro-vides us with more clues as to the true nature of the original images; slowly but surely, we piece the "whole story" together. The soundtrack reconfirms this suspense feeling; once the ocean sounds have decayed past recogni-tion, the remaining configuration of electrons on the tape create an eerie, dangerous-sounding accompaniment. In general, "A Wind" reworks a strat-egy mentioned earlier in connection with Snow and Gehr: the conventional structure of viewer reception – the gradual but relentless build toward climax (in this case, the "climax" of being able to identify the images) and dé-nouement (here, the prints of "A Wind" we see after we've made the iden-tifications) – is retained but used to reveal subject matter that represents an inversion of convention.

While the suspense-thriller dimension of *Print Generation* ends several print generations before the conclusion of "A Wind," the film's revelations about its original subject of inquiry – the degree to which making prints of imagery destroys or distorts its impact and meaning – are especially revealing near the end of "A Wind" (and again at the beginning of "B Wind"). In many cases, it is only during the last three, or two, generations of "A Wind" that important nuances of an image are even visible: The rain in a shot of a backyard in the rain, for example, is apparent for only the final two generations in "A Wind" and the first two in "B Wind"; it is invisible in the remaining forty-six. And, of course, the specifics of color are affected by only one or two generations, the blues and browns most notably.

Ironically, while Murphy's experimental procedure was devised to examine issues that are "covered" rather definitively in the last ten minutes of "A Wind" and the first ten minutes of "B Wind," the process of "excavating" layer by layer up and down through the layers of color discovered new forms of imagery that exist not only outside conventional viewers' awareness but *underneath* the imagery they do see, buried by it. The most interesting of these new forms of imagery are evident about halfway through "A Wind" and "B Wind": semi-identifiable places and figures in trembling configurations of gorgeous scarlet. Of course, within the context of *Print Generation,* this imagery (and the various other forms of imagery excavated by Murphy's process) creates a paradox; though it is evidence of a form of extreme decay dozens of generations from the original, it is at the same time, almost entirely *un*decayed, since in *Murphy*'s film it is a first-generation print (a print made from the *Print Generation* original). Murphy's film foregrounds elements of cinema that viewers usually ignore, increasing viewers' awareness of them by exaggerating the conventional process of decay, *and then* transforms these exaggerations of cinematic entropy into their opposite.

Murphy's exploration of the conditions of viewership occurs on other levels as well. One of these is a function of viewers' attempts to identify the various images as they form, print by print. During the first ten minutes or so of "A Wind," the imagery is something like a Rorschach test. The configurations of dots of color are so abstract that attempts to identify the imagery reveal at least as much about viewer psychology as they do about the original images the dots are vestiges of. Is it purely accidental that of the sixty images, the image identified first by a very high percentage of people is of a woman walking (Murphy's *mother* no less)? Or does it reveal something about our fundamental cultural conditioning; after all, for most members of most modern cultures and probably ancient cultures as well, a walking woman (a walking *mother*) is probably the first moving image the eye and mind recognize. The second image viewers of *Print Generation* seem to recognize is a child toddling across a yard. From this point on, responses seem more varied, though several flowers in a breeze in close-up, a man sawing wood, and several faces are images that trigger early identification, or at least more accurate guesses. I expect that a more precise investigation of the details of audience response to *Print Generation* might reveal a good bit about the nature and history of our responses to motion. In other words, Murphy's film invites viewers to study the motion of their own consciousness, especially the process of their apprehension of visual information.

Once viewers have realized that all of the one-second bits of imagery in Murphy's grid are, at some point, likely to be identifiable, a second level of questioning develops that often reveals their cultural training as film viewers. As *Print Generation* moves layer by layer up through the emulsion, more and more of the space delimited by the frames is covered by color and light. The tendency of most viewers is to project onto the forming imagery locations familiar from our conventional film experiences. Indeed, since the tiny, cohering dots of emulsion "dance" and since their dance fills the entire frame – rather than the center of the image, where most conventional action occurs – the earliest of these projections tend toward the

Murphy's mother, from *Print Generation.*

spectacular. Viewers "see" cities, amusement parks, busy oceanfront board-walks at night, scenes reminiscent of the pleasures of childhood and of the film spectaculars through which many children are introduced to popular cinema.

By the end of "A Wind," viewers' spectacular expectations have been undercut: Most of the images document Murphy's trips to Vermont to see filmmaker/friend Norman Bloom and to visit his mother at her home in Bayonne, New Jersey. Once one recognizes the images as diaristic, the min-ute-by-minute "journey" toward the scenes and people Murphy experienced in the summer of 1973 can be seen as a reflection of a young filmmaker's excitement about being part of a growing alternative cinema. From the perspective of 1974, the beginnings of cinema and the conventional indus-trial spectacles they had paved the way for must have seemed part of larger developments that were now taking cinema history more fully in the direc-tion of *personal* expression and communication, as evinced by the wide range of "personal cinema" produced in the 1960s and early 1970s. Of course, as is usually the case, this movement forward was simultaneously a return to the past: as has been suggested, Murphy's sixty diary images (each seen for a total of fifty seconds during the film) are reminiscent of the Lumières, just as his grid organization and study of movement are remi-niscent of Muybridge.

So far, I have centered this discussion on the first half of *Print Generation*. But "B Wind" does more than reconfirm "A Wind." "B Wind" tests the memory. As the imagery decays, print by print, it quickly reverts to the form it was in, prior to viewers being able to identify it; and, in a surprising number of cases, they are quickly puzzled once again, unable to remember what this particular configuration became. As "B Wind" continues, one is as likely to remember inaccurate guesses as the correct identifications. An-other result of Murphy's inclusion of "B Wind" is an undercutting of the conventional, orgasmic, narrative shape "A Wind" (like *Wavelength* and *Serene Velocity*) implicitly reiterates. *Print Generation* is perfectly sym-metrical; in fact, its "dénouement" is as long as its development: Murphy shows us *all* the results of his experiment and leaves us to discover whatever entertainment we need, a decision reminiscent of Muybridge's decision to use his method for recording animal and human motion for many more particular subjects than anyone would be likely to study in detail.

The experience of *Print Generation* not only provides still another re-contextualization of conventional moviegoing, it implicitly situates this par-ticular experience within the multilayered processes that have brought viewers into the theater, including their development as children (and their acculturation as film viewers) and the more general evolutionary developments that have fashioned the essential structures of human existence. That *Print Generation* begins with individual, isolated particles of emulsion that slowly cohere into increasingly complex forms may be more than a metaphor for the origin of life and the evolution of species and societies. Since these original, trembling particles are the result of the impact of light on a chemical substance, they seem almost a vestige of the miracle out of which all life and consciousness have developed. Of course, the fact that *Print Generation* ends by delivering viewers back to those original particles is a warning that the moment of any particular film experience (and of the lives it records/ dramatizes), and the historical "moment" of cinema itself, are no more than metaphors for the evolutionary moment in which we find ourselves and which is disappearing even as we experience it.

NOTES

1. Murphy discusses the thinking that led to and through *Print Generation* in Scott MacDonald, *A Critical Cinema* (Berkeley, CA: University of California Press, 1988), pp. 183–8.
2. *Print Generation* recalls in particular Ian Burn's *Xerox Book* (1968), which Murphy saw in Ursula Meyer's *Conceptual Art* (New York: Dutton, 1972), pp. 94–5.

5
Morgan Fisher
Standard Gauge

Morgan Fisher has been making films for approximately as long as the other filmmakers discussed in this section: The four earliest films listed in his filmography – *The Director and His Actor Look at Footage Showing Preparations for an Unmade Film (2), Documentary Footage, Phi Phenomenon,* and *Screening Room* – were completed in 1968. But while his films have many things in common with those previously discussed, his stance toward conventional cinema, and toward the Hollywood industry in particular, has always been different from theirs. Like these other filmmakers, Fisher has critiqued the products of the film industry, but, unlike them, Fisher has been an active, direct participant in the process of commercial movie making during the same period. In the early 1970s, Fisher worked as an editor on several low-budget features, including Roger Corman's *The Student Nurses* (1970), and he did stock footage research for a never-completed Haskell Wexler film that was to follow *Medium Cool* (1969). These and other related experiences have had a powerful effect on Fisher and on the way he understands his position as independent filmmaker.[1] Instead of seeing himself as detached from the world of conventional film commerce, Fisher has used the process of making avant-garde films as a way of examining what he has learned about film from working in the industry. For Fisher, avant-garde film isn't simply a separate arena of film practice, it *derives from* commercial film and, paradoxically, its derivative status gives it a unique capability to critique the film world that generated it. The result has been a series of films as unconventional as those discussed in earlier chapters, but unconventional in a somewhat different way.

From the moment he began to make films, Fisher – like Gehr and Murphy – was interested in the historical and technological conditions of film. Fisher has frequently extended the Lumière approach into long single-shot movies,

54

or into films made up entirely of a series of continuous roll-long shots; and he has not only filmically studied Muybridge (he was Thom Andersen's primary assistant on *Eadweard Muybridge, Zoopraxographer* (1974), an intelligent and informative biography of the photographer's career), he has paid homage to him (actually, to Muybridge and the Lumières) in *Documentary Footage*, a single-shot film, exactly one 300-foot roll of 16mm film long (eleven minutes) in which a naked woman (her nakedness an allusion to the nakedness of the people photographed in Muybridge's motion studies) is filmed, first, as she reads and tape records a series of questions about her body, pausing after each question, and then, having rewound the tape recorder, as she answers the questions during the pauses. In *Documentary Footage* we can study the motion of the woman's body, *and* her changing relation to the camera/tape recorder and her prospective future audience, as she responds to Fisher's various directorial assignments. In general, Fisher's films use long, continuous shots to make various types of motion study possible, whether the "motion" presented is a particular human or mechanical action, the production of a film (as in *Production Stills*, 1970), or the history of an aspect of Fisher's career (as in *Standard Gauge*, 1984). In *Production Stills* and *Standard Gauge*, in fact, individual still images of a process are mounted and implicitly compared.

All the filmmakers discussed in this section make films that have complex conceptual dimensions. Ono in particular was seminal in the development of what came to be known as conceptual art and, to some degree, Snow, Gehr, and Murphy affected and/or were affected by it. Fisher's films are at least as fully conceptual as any of the films discussed so far. In fact, while all of Fisher's films have a minimal elegance, this look is simply a means for making sure that viewers will not be distracted from the films' complex conceptual designs. The most consistent conceptual tactic Fisher employs is paradox. Most every film develops a set of paradoxes that grow increasingly intricate, the more viewers think about what they're seeing and the more they know about the worlds of industry and avant-garde filmmaking. The fact that Fisher's films declare themselves only to those willing to *think* about them is their most fundamental critique of conventional cinema and its tendency to assume that thinking is precisely what viewers go to the movies to escape.

In some instances – *Phi Phenomenon* and *Screening Room*, for example – Fisher has used paradox to explore particular dimensions of cinema technology that underlie both conventional and avant-garde film practice, in the way Gehr and Murphy do in *Serene Velocity* and *Print Generation*. In most of his films, however, Fisher's explorations of the cinematic apparatus

55

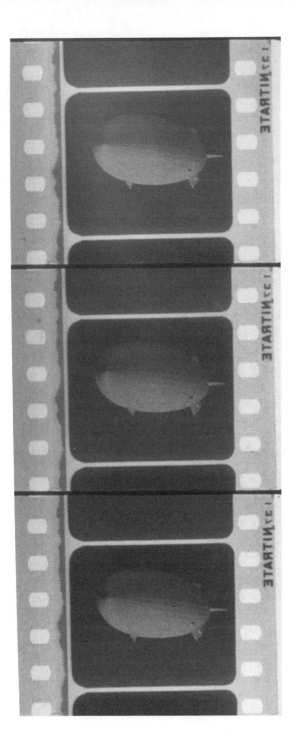

reflect his unusual status as both avant-garde filmmaker and industry employee. In *Production Stills*, for example, he redirects industry equipment for filming on a sound stage (a Mitchell camera on a Moviola crab dolly) so that it records no dramatic emotional scene played by actors, but a series of eight black and white Polaroids, mounted one by one on a portion of white wall in front of the camera, on a continuous 300-foot roll of 16mm film. The central function of a soundstage, of course, is the production of seamless sync sound records of actors speaking their lines but, in *Production Stills* we must deduce that the image and sound are synchronized from hearing that the sound of the Polaroid camera taking each Polaroid is "in sync" with the slight lightening of the image as a result of the flash bulbs. Voices are heard, but offscreen. Paradoxically, these voices are not those of actors in the conventional sense, but of "behind-the-scenes" technicians, who in *this* film become both crew *and* cast, "performing" their usual functions in a double sense that simultaneously confirms and defies the conventional hierarchy of industry film production. As the title indicates, the Polaroids themselves are production stills of the process being used to film the Polaroids and record the sync soundtrack. Fisher uses a combination of avant-garde and industry procedures (a long single shot and a serial organization; industry equipment) to refocus both cinematic worlds: An avant-garde film asks viewers to meditate on the workings of the commercial industry; industry equipment is used to subvert the conventional meaning of production stills, which are conventionally a means to an end – the marketing of a commercial narrative feature – but here are the subject of the film itself.

In general, Fisher's films are metaphors for the idea that the next step in the direction of a more thorough and effective critical cinema is a conscious synthesis of the advantages of the commercial industry and the insights of avant-garde filmmaking. His most elaborate demonstration of this idea is *Standard Gauge*, which at thirty-five minutes is by far his longest film. It's Fisher's "epic" in both length and scope.

Standard Gauge focuses on that element of the cinematic apparatus which, more than any other perhaps, distinguishes the commercial cinema from the avant-garde. Generally speaking, conventional films are shot and printed on 35mm film stock – that is, on "standard gauge" – and avant-garde films are shot on 16mm, or on narrower gauges. After a brief prologue in the

---

Three consecutive frames of Morgan Fisher's *Standard Gauge* (1984). The 35mm filmstrip pictured suggests a parallel between two flammable technologies: nitrate stock and hydrogen zeppelins.

form of a rolling text (itself an allusion to the use of textual prologues in epic commercial films) that explains the derivation of 35mm as the "standard gauge" of conventional cinema, Fisher presents a series of strips of 35mm film he has collected over the years and discusses the circumstances of his acquiring them. While the ostensible subject is the strips, the fundamental issue is the interface between standard-gauge and 16mm film, and the filmic forms they are normally used for. The strips of 35mm film are an index of the commercial industry, and they are presented by means of a homemade light table meant to convey the sense that Fisher and the viewer are "eye-balling" footage on an editing table. Each strip is threaded into this device and stopped on particular frames. While the focus is on remnants of the industry, however, these remnants are recorded and presented with 16mm equipment. And they are never seen as they were meant to be seen. We always see the frames *and* the strips on which they're printed. We can't experience their original motion, only their motion as strips within the 16mm recording.

As is suggested by the title – and by Fisher's narration – commercial filmmaking is the source of basic film technology and procedures that trickle down to other filmmakers and audiences in the form of smaller gauges. But Fisher demonstrates that the development of a smaller, nonstandard gauge has paradoxically provided filmmakers with options not available in the wider gauge. Most obviously, 16mm allows for a thirty-two-minute continuous shot, a shot longer than 35mm cameras are capable of making – and long enough to allow Fisher to present the strips of 35mm without interruption. As *Standard Gauge* develops, the larger temporal capacity of the smaller gauge becomes a metaphor for the opportunity provided by 16mm for an extended critique of conventional film history, an opportunity implicit in the title. "Standard Gauge" does refer to the industry (may even imply an homage), but it is simultaneously a rebellion against the industry. It is doubtful that an industry entertainment would ever be called "Standard Gauge": Only an avant-garde film would be likely to use a title that requires some particular knowledge of equipment and materials, even something as basic as the definition of "gauge."

Standard Gauge presents Fisher's collection of 35mm filmstrips as a series of specimens to be analyzed by 16mm filmgoers. But while the 35mm filmstrips are, in a general sense, an index of the industry, Fisher's particular choice of filmstrips for the film is also an index of his rebellion against conventional filmmaking, on at least two levels. First, the filmstrips and the narration about them develop a set of references to traditions of filmmaking within the industry that have rebelled against its standard assumptions, as well as references to avant-garde critiques. Second, Fisher's presentation and discussion of particular details of some of the filmstrips reveal dimensions of the industry that normally remain invisible because of the industry's assumptions about how films should be experienced by the audience.

Though *Standard Gauge* defines Fisher as essentially, primarily an avant-garde filmmaker (by being made in 16mm, using a variety of avant-garde procedures), it paradoxically pays homage to those filmmakers who have worked to redirect the industry from within its ranks, or, if not from within Hollywood, at least in 35mm. The first filmstrip presented and discussed in Fisher's narration is a piece of leader discarded during the subtitling of Godard's *La Chinoise* (1967). Godard's journey from critic to (French) industry filmmaker to Marxist independent epitomizes one 35mm response to industry convention. Fisher also discusses strips from Corman's *Student Nurses* and from *Blood Virgin* (a.k.a. *The Second Coming* and *Messiah of Evil*), written by Gloria Katz and Willard Huyck and directed by Huyck; and he describes an inventive shot near the end of Edgar J. Ulmer's *Detour* (1946). These references are reminders of the B-movie tradition that allowed some commercial directors to express themselves and at times critique their more monied, industry colleagues. Fisher's narration ends with an unexplained reference to *The Honeymoon Killers* (c. 1970), the only film by Vernon Castle, who spent his life working in the industry on others' films. The ingenuity of Castle's film, according to Fisher (it is not in distribution), epitomizes the potential of even nondirectors working within the industry to surprise the expectations developed by their history as industry employees. Paradoxically, Fisher's unexplained reference to this film would make sense only to those familiar enough with the industry to recognize the implications of the allusion, that is to say, to very few of those who would attend a screening of a 16mm avant-garde film. The mysterious reference is meant to entice those in the avant-garde audience toward this proof that the industry produces rebels within its own ranks.[2]

Fisher's filmstrips not only reference the particular films (and TV shows) they are remnants of, they also encode particular industry equipment, materials, and processes – and the people in charge of them. As a result of his history as part of the industry, Fisher is empathetic with the industry's working class, including those thousands of people in charge of developing and maintaining industry standards, but normally beyond the ken of most conventional (and avant-garde) film audiences, and often not even identified in the credits, except indirectly as part of a company employed by the producers. The issue of the invisibility of these contributors to conventional cinema is raised even before the body of *Standard Gauge*, during the rolling text with which the film begins. We learn that Edison employee W. K. L. Dickson, who had been the crucial figure in the Edison Laboratory's development of motion picture technology, was the person primarily responsible for determining that film would be 1⅜ (or approximately 35mm) wide. Despite his contributions, however, it is not his name that is recognized by the public as the originator of American cinematic technology, but the name of the Edison company that employed him. The same issue is implicit in the fact that while we can see Fisher's light box being threaded with each strip of 35mm film, we cannot see his hands doing the threading, a metaphor for the many people who work around the edges of the industry to make possible what we see in the frame.

During Fisher's presentation of his collection of 35mm film strips, a host of normally invisible contributors to the production of commercial films are remembered. Each group is identified with one or more of the mysterious markings that decorate the heads and tails of reels of film – the celluloid margins that usually remain outside the vision and awareness of moviegoers when films are projected. Fisher's narrative begins with comments about the friend who prepared the English subtitles for *La Chinoise*. The particular film strips Fisher discusses are pieces of head and tail leader onto which subtitles from a previous or subsequent shot have run. Fittingly, given Fisher's subsequent comments about the usually anonymous laborers who work with film, several of these subtitles refer to issues of class: "In the West the Imperialists are still oppressing...," for example. Other workers are introduced when Fisher reviews his experience working at a stock footage library and his return, years later, to talk with the librarians there about getting a print of a particular image. Still others who seem marginal to film audiences, but are quite central to the production of movies, are implied by Fisher's memories of working as second editor on *Student Nurses,* by his comments about the Technicolor workers whom he met at a Technicolor lab in Hollywood, and by those "Friends of I.B." who published a poignant memorial announcement to imbibition (I.B.) printing: "In Loving Memory, I.B. Born 1927 – Died 1975. Hollywood's own dye transfer process whose life was unrivaled for beauty, longevity, and flexibility. We salute you."

A final group of Hollywood's usually invisible working class is introduced in Fisher's comments about the use of the China Girl, the images of women dressed in multicolored clothes that are often seen on heads and tails of reels of film. The China Girl's function is to act as a color-control standard: The skin-tone of white skin is the norm against which other colors are measured. Fisher's presentation of a series of China Girls references two groups of laborers, "the people working behind the scenes, such as laboratory technicians, those people who dedicate their lives to rendering appearance perfect, who know these women best," and the women themselves.

Fisher's comments about the China Girl raise another issue closely related to the industry's exploitation of its anonymous working class. In general, women have remained on the margins of the film industry, except as images to be gazed at. For Fisher, the China Girl is emblematic of this situation: "This figure's sex, her being in the margin of the film, her serving to establish and maintain a standard of correct appearance...are aspects of a single question that deserves thought." The degree to which the film history Fisher reviews is gendered is also implicit in the fact that the only other women mentioned during his narration are figures within the films Fisher worked on: the student nurses, the owner of an art gallery in *Blood Virgin*. Of course, the fact that the China Girl's white skin serves as the industry standard suggests the even more thorough marginalization of people of

"SCENE MISSING" (which is cut into an industry workprint when there's an insert to be added later) becomes its opposite in Fisher's *Standard Gauge*.

color, both as actors within conventional films and as members of the working-class surround of the industry's glamorous productions. In *Standard Gauge,* Fisher uses the capabilities of 16mm to cinematically demarginalize the contributions of the industry's working class and the issues implied by their marginalization. He enables us to read and understand the celluloid evidence of the input of these contributors, evidence the industry consistently suppresses, at least visually, as part of its overall goal of causing its products to have the impact of magical incarnations.

While Fisher is well aware of the class, gender, and racial suppressions of the industry, however, he is not satisfied merely to provide a detached critique of these conditions. An essential paradox of *Standard Gauge* is that the pertinence of Fisher's critical insights does not overshadow his respect for the institution he critiques. Fisher is well aware that no matter how fully he might disapprove of one or another dimension of the industry's methods of production or its products, he remains grateful for the pleasure the industry has given him and proud of his connections with it. The strips of film *Standard Gauge* centers on are not simply evidence of ideological shortcomings; they are treated as beloved souvenirs of an institution in economic decline that, despite its shortcomings, must be mourned.[3]

Of course, the best evidence of Fisher's pride in his connections to the industry is his decision to focus many of his films, including his longest, on it. Fisher is well aware that the development of the industry and of an elaborate set of conventional audience expectations has made a critical cinema not only of interest, not only of considerable classroom use, but *possible. Standard Gauge* demonstrates this relationship during Fisher's discussion of his return to the stock-footage library. The industry newsreel image he returned to retrieve was a shot of an execution of a Fascist prison superintendent, the same shot "that appears in Bruce Conner's film *A Movie* [1958]." Fisher is unable to afford to have the lab make a print of the scene, and to ease his disappointment, one of the technicians hands him a piece of nitrate film. It turns out to be the two different images of the *Hindenburg* (the image on screen during this story and a second, which Fisher subsequently shows us), "the very dirigible that is seen in the Conner film in the throes of an apocalyptic catastrophe." Without small-gauge reproductions of industry film, Conner couldn't have made *A Movie,* the film that established Conner's reputation as an avant-garde pioneer, and, in the long run, inspired the "found-footage film" we're watching. Paradoxically, the industry's economic dominance, which mitigates against independent film production, both necessitated Conner's ingenuity and supplied him with the raw materials out of which he was to develop a telling film-critical career.

Similarly paradoxical relationships exist on the level of genre. It is *because* industry genres are conventionally impersonal – in the sense that whatever one learns about a film's makers from a genre film is, at best, disguised and deflected – that the avant-garde's tradition of personal cinema can function as a form of critique. In *Standard Gauge,* Fisher's revelation of his personal involvements with the industry is only interesting because of the industry's conventional impersonality. Of course, Fisher's personalness is itself a paradox, since he is personal only about his industry work life, not about what we normally consider a personal life – a pattern that reiterates the industry even as it critiques it, and defies the avant-garde, even as it reconfirms it. The industry's "impersonality" is also paradoxical, in the sense that the personal lives of the stars (whose lives really aren't personal at all, at least insofar as we know about them) are often largely responsible for the economic success of the industry's "impersonal" products.

For Fisher, the current interest of cinema history is neither the industry's production of a cinema of pervasive popular impact nor the avant-garde's development of a varied and fascinating set of critical alternatives to the industry but, rather, the potential for an ongoing dialectic between these two cinematic worlds that has the potential for moving both in new, more progressive directions. Fisher's journey through the history of the industry and through his own experiences as a contributor to it is, in the final analysis, a means for defying the current distinction between these two cinematic "geographies," for moving through the traditional boundary between them. *Standard Gauge* proposes, as Fisher explains in a synopsis of the film, "a kind of mutuality or interdependence between two kinds of filmmaking that by conventional standards are thought to be divided by an unbridgeable chasm. By means of a mutual interrogation between 35mm, the gauge of the industry, and 16mm, the gauge of the independent and amateur, *Standard Gauge* proposes to unify film of every kind."[4] *Standard Gauge* might not appeal to a much larger sector of the conventional audience than *Serene Velocity* or *Print Generation,* but it aims for a more diverse audience, made up, paradoxically, of those who know the industry from the inside *and* who critique it from an avant-garde distance.

NOTES

1. Fisher discusses his double identity as contributor to the Hollywood industry and independent filmmaker in Scott MacDonald, *A Critical Cinema* (Berkeley, CA: University of California Press, 1988), pp. 356–73.

2. Fisher talked about *The Honeymoon Killers* in a phone conversation on April 30, 1991. Thanks to Jim Hoberman for additional information.

3. *Standard Gauge* provides considerable evidence that, for those in the West, the industry's golden days are behind us: The sale of the I.B. Technicolor process to the People's Republic of China, a sale that is a direct result of the increasing economic unfeasibility of making first-rate movie color, is an obvious instance.

4. The unpublished synopsis was written for the New York Film Festival when *Standard Gauge* was shown there in 1985.

Part II
Psychic Excursions

In terms of the content they explore, the temporal and spatial organization they use, and the types of viewer engagement they promote, commercial directors are generally predictable; in fact, it is their ingenuity in exploiting and reenergizing traditional narrative forms that makes them commercial. Some of the most inventive critical filmmakers of recent decades have set out to surprise the expectations developed by the history of conventional film narrative and to develop new, ideologically more progressive forms of narrative enjoyment. Part 2 discusses five critiques of commercial film's fetishization of a particular, limited range of narrative procedures. In general, the films focus on aspects of human development that are marginalized or elided in commercial movies; and all five encourage unconventional modes of filmmaker/film/audience interaction.

In *Zorns Lemma*, Hollis Frampton uses a highly formalized structure to take viewers on a journey from innocence and ignorance to maturity and enlightenment. Each of the film's three sections creates a form of audience involvement that functions as a metaphor for one of the stages of intellectual growth Frampton and his audience have presumably experienced. Whereas the destination of *Zorns Lemma* is intellectual enlightenment in general, the destination of *Riddles of the Sphinx* is more specific: a more extensive and effective awareness of the problematic gender definitions that inform the history of modern society (and conventional cinema). The struggle of the film's protagonist to move from inside the nuclear family out into the world is confirmed by the film's difficulty for most viewers. The unusual structure of *Riddles of the Sphinx* is a way of challenging and training viewers to become more fully engaged in progressive cultural redefinitions. The structure of *American Dreams* encourages viewers to read themselves into the psyche of a macho protagonist, as a means of developing a more

65

thorough sense of the implications of conventional macho thinking. The relentlessness of James Benning's structure creates an experience that is simultaneously critique and index of a conventionally masculine way of approaching experience. *The Ties That Bind* develops an identification between audience and filmmaker/protagonist Su Friedrich, as she uses the making of a film to develop a new relationship with her mother and their shared past. Formally, her unconventional combination of diverse kinds of cinematic information and her development of a network of subtle interconnections between image and non-sync sound model the process of breaking through conventional barriers to create constructive relationships. Finally, in *From the Pole to the Equator,* Yervant Gianikian and Angela Ricci Lucchi retrieve important relics from the cinematic past (the collected films of early Italian cinematographer/explorer Luca Comerio) and restructure them so that the experience of seeing Comerio's imagery simultaneously reveals the cinema's (and the cinema audience's) complicity in the history of imperial domination of nonindustrialized peoples and provides a far more humane view of Comerio's subjects than he seems to have been interested in providing.

6

Hollis Frampton
Zorns Lemma

Like several of the films discussed in Part 1, Hollis Frampton's films are radically different from conventional movies, not only because of their minimal content and the nature of their systematic structures, but in their "address" to the viewer. As is true of most critical films, Frampton's films provide experiences most conventional viewers would consider entirely non-filmic, *with no indication that anything out of the ordinary is occurring.* Of course, like the films discussed in Part 1, Frampton's films were not made with the idea of their being available to conventional moviegoers in conventional circumstances. I would guess Frampton made his films for himself (or, as Gertrude Stein, a Frampton favorite, might say, for himself and a few friends) in the hope that some larger part of the art world would discover them later. But even those who might see these films at a specialized screening room would be confronted by much the same "problem" more conventional viewers would face: Unlike conventional film directors whose ability to function within the industry requires that their films create at least the illusion of accessibility and clarity, the illusion that viewers know all they need to, Frampton did not hesitate to make use of types of information few moviegoers of any type would be conversant with, and he did so with no explanation whatsoever – apparently on the assumption that filmgoers can be expected to do research.

Even a partial understanding of Frampton's films requires a rudimentary sense of the history of mathematics, science, and technology and of the literary and fine arts. *Maxwell's Demon* (1968), for example, is an homage to physicist James Clerk Maxwell, "father of thermodynamics and analytic color theory"; *Prince Ruperts Drops* (1969) gets its title from a demonstration done in physics classrooms; *States* (1967, 1970) is edited according to a system derived from what mathematics calls the Fibonacci series (in

which each member is the sum of the previous two). The structure of *Palindrome* (1969) was a conscious application to film of musical principles explored by the composer Webern; and the content and structure of later Frampton films owe a good deal to James Joyce and Gertrude Stein. Nowhere is Frampton's assumption that his viewers can be expected to be informed, or to inform themselves, more obvious than in *Zorns Lemma*, the challenging film that established Frampton as a major contributor to alternative cinema.

Zorns Lemma combines several areas of intellectual and esthetic interest Frampton had explored in his early photographic work and in his early films. His fascination with mathematics, and in particular with set theory – explicit in his generation of numerical sets as a way of determining the placement of imagery in *States* and *Heterodyne* (1967), and implicit in his use of a deck of playing cards as a system for the photographic series, *The Secret World of Frank Stella* (1958–62)[1] – is the source of the title *Zorns Lemma*. Mathematician Max Zorn's "lemma," the eleventh axiom of set theory, proposes that, given a set of sets, there is a further set composed of a representative item from each set. *Zorns Lemma* doesn't exactly demonstrate Zorn's lemma, but Frampton's allusion to the "existential axiom" is appropriate, given his use of a set of sets to structure the film. Frampton's longtime interest in languages and literature is equally evident in *Zorns Lemma*. In the brief opening section of the film the viewer watches a dark screen as a woman reads verses from the *Bay State Primer* (Euro-America's first English grammar text) that highlight words beginning with the successive letters of the Roman alphabet: "In *A*dam's fall we sinned all"; "Thy life to mend, God's *B*ook attend"; "The *C*at doth play, and after slay" . . . (italics added). And the film's long second section begins with set after set of alphabetically arranged environmental words.

Once the voice has finished reading the verses from the *Bay State Primer*, Frampton begins the second section with a run-through of a twenty-four-letter version of the Roman alphabet (*U* and *V*, *I* and *J* are considered the same letters), against a black background, one second per letter – a temporal rhythm maintained throughout the remainder of the film. During the forty-seven minutes of the second section, the viewer at first sees (this section is silent) set after set of alphabetically arranged words recorded in locations all over lower Manhattan (each set is separated from the next by one second

---

The replacement image for *E*; an homage to the old Fox Theater in Flatbush (an *F* image); and the replacement image for *V*, from the second section of Hollis Frampton's *Zorns Lemma* (1970).

69

of darkness). The words are not arranged so that they make sense together (the rare conjunction of successive words – "limp" "member," in the thirty-second set, for example – is the exception that proves that Frampton's rule was to avoid combining words). The overall experience is of a phantasmagoria of environmental language. Although the basic one-second rhythm of the section never changes, the experience of the sets of words is far from uniform and regular. The location of particular words within the frame and their material presentation (the nature of the words themselves, the specific movements of Frampton's hand-held camera, and the environment in which the words are seen) are continually changing so that the eye's exploration of successive shots functions as a counterpoint to the one-shot-per-second meter. As more and more repetitions of alphabetized words are presented, the formal properties of certain sets of words become motifs: For example, there is a set of superimposed words and a set of words seen in paper collages constructed by Frampton.

Once viewers have begun to grow accustomed to the relentless alphabetic organization, Frampton institutes a second procedure that in the end transforms the section. One-second successive bits of ongoing phenomena or activities are gradually substituted for the one-second environmental words. The first four substitution images are a large bonfire at night (for the letter X), ocean waves breaking on a beach (for Z), a tracking shot of weeds (for Y), and steam escaping from a street vent (for Q) – a reference to the four classic elements: fire, water, earth, air. Most later substitutions involve people accomplishing various everyday tasks – a close-up of hands turning the pages of a book (A), hands grinding hamburger (I/J), three construction workers digging a hole (M), a man (Robert Huot) painting a wall (K), a man (Frampton) changing a tire (T) – and still others reveal animals and plants: two rhinoceri (S), a red ibis flapping its wings (C), a single tree in winter (F). In nearly all instances in which people are seen accomplishing particular tasks, the tasks are placed within *Zorns Lemma* so that they are completed precisely when the second section is complete. For some viewers, a good bit of suspense develops during the latter stages of the section about which letter will be replaced next, and, at the very end, at what point the final substitution will bring the entire set of developments to a close.

If the second section of *Zorns Lemma* is Muybridgian – not only in its general use of the serial, but because the one-second bits of the replacement images "analyze" continuous activities or motions in a manner analogous to Muybridge's motion studies – the final section is Lumièresque. For eleven minutes we watch a man (Robert Huot), a woman (Marcia Steinbrecher), and a dog walk across a snowy field, beginning near the camera and moving

70

directly away from the camera down across a small valley, then up toward and into a distant woods. The walk takes nearly four complete 100-foot rolls of film spliced together so that, although the pauses between rolls are visible, the film creates the sense of a long continuous shot. After the couple has entered the woods, the final roll flares to white. On the soundtrack six female voices read a portion of *On Light, or the Ingression of Forms,* a metaphysical explanation of the structure of the world by Robert Grosseteste (Bishop of Lincoln during the eleventh century), alternating voices one word at a time, in synchronization with a metronome:

The/first/bodily/form/I/judge/to/be/Light. . . .

The tripartite structure of *Zorns Lemma* can be understood in various ways, at least two of them roughly suggestive of early film history. The progression from darkness, to individual one-second units of imagery, to long, continuous shots is reminiscent of what Frampton may have seen as the movement from no experiences of animated motion, to the brief bits of illusory motion created by nineteenth-century philosophical toys and by Muybridge's use of the Zoopraxiscope, to the Edison and Lumière cameras/ projectors that made extended moving images possible. When sound is taken into consideration, the progression may suggest the development from sound technology (the Edison labs had developed the phonograph before Edison conceived of motion pictures as a potentially marketable accompaniment to phonograph discs) to silent film (and the silent era's development of increasingly sophisticated editing strategies) to the coming of sound film (and Bazinian commitment to the continuous shot).

The most fruitful approach to the progression, however, is to see it as a narrative mapping of human intellectual development. This approach accounts not only for the film's particular imagery and sound, but for the unusual experience the film creates for viewers. Essentially, the three sections of *Zorns Lemma* correspond to three phases of life – childhood, youth or young adulthood, and maturity – phases that are often characterized by different forms of intellectual process. Frampton places the viewer in relationships to imagery and sound that are analogous to the successive phases of development.

In the opening passage, for example, viewers are in a dark room waiting for imagery to be projected, listening to a narrator read a series of verses – an experience Frampton sees as analogous to the intellectual experience of childhood. Frampton's view of his/our first years is the diametric opposite of Stan Brakhage's. Whereas Brakhage was for a time consumed by what he saw as the wonders of childhood vision (vision "under childhood," before verbal training has begun to limit what and how we see), Frampton sees childhood as a time of darkness, a period of near stasis during which nothing of importance is seen and almost nothing understood. The basic situation of a woman reading verses, and from *The Bay State Primer* in particular, recalls those early months when an adult reading to a child is a central form of interchange that has as much to do with passing on accepted moral and religious lessons as with transferring to the child the intellectual tools necessary for effectively exploring the world (in the *Bay State Primer* verses, the alphabet – the supposed pretext for the verses – is, for all practical purposes, buried within the religious references). The schoolmarmish voice of the woman suggests a period when the adults in charge of a child's education are primarily important as disciplinarians and the earliest lessons have mostly to do with what happens when rules are disobeyed.

For Frampton, the development of verbal skills doesn't destroy visual innocence; it releases the child from the prison of ignorance and indoctrination. Immediately following the completion of *The Bay State Primer* verses, *Zorns Lemma* jumps into the energetic image-per-second rhythm it maintains until the final moments of the film. This sudden, dramatic change is Frampton's way of recreating for the audience some sense of the experience of moving from a time when children are intellectually cloistered into a period when the acquisition of basic verbal/linguistic skills enables them to codify and understand the world, and to enter new realms of experience.

Frampton's decision to use a twenty-four-letter version of the Roman alphabet, rather than the twenty-six-letter modern alphabet, also makes sense in a context of the educational process. The choice seems an obvious allusion to the fact that each second of sound film is composed of twenty-four frames, and a way of emphasizing that each alphabetic set is composed of a set of sets of film frames. The film's continual reiteration of the alphabet is, on one level, a reminder of a process almost all of us experienced during our early years in school. On another level, the extended parallel between the alphabetic set and the individual second of the film suggest that *Zorns Lemma* is a new, cinematic schooling, where viewers are learning to understand the organization of *this* film and, by implication, discovering that there are many more ways of constructing a film experience than their conventional viewing experiences have prepared them for.

During the second section of *Zorns Lemma*, Frampton explores a longer and more elaborate period of intellectual growth. Not surprisingly, the visual imagery is much more various and complex than the auditory imagery presented in the film's opening passage, and the audience's position with regard to this imagery is correspondingly challenging. At first, the experience of seeing the sets of environmental words is a rush, particularly since there's a tendency not only to see the words and recognize their position in the alphabetic order, but to try to explore the environment within which each word is filmed. Frampton makes this process intriguing by filming the words in a wide variety of circumstances. Often, he films words printed on or exhibited inside of the windows of businesses so that other imagery is seen with the word or so that the imagery reflected by the window surfaces is superimposed over the verbal "content" of particular shots. Although the repeated alphabetic sets provide a regular, simple structure for hundreds of brief shots, the varied spaces that surround the words render the audience's experience roughly akin to the Odessa Steps section of Eisenstein's *Potemkin* (a passage Frampton had burlesqued in an earlier film).[2]

As set after set of alphabetized words and their environments is experienced, it is difficult not to develop a sense of Frampton's experience making the film. The film's collection of hundreds of environmental words suggests that the film was a labor of love, and an index of the filmmaker's extended travels around lower Manhattan, looking for, finding, and recording the words. In fact, the film's serial organization forms a grid against which we can measure Frampton's motions as filmmaker collecting the units that form the grid.

Once viewers notice that Frampton has begun to replace the environmental words with the one-second bits of continuing activities, the experience of the second section becomes very different. When I have taught *Zorns Lemma,* I have often asked students if they can remember which replacement image was substituted for each letter, and I have discovered that a good many viewers consciously memorize the correspondences. For most viewers the experience of "learning" the correspondences is fatiguing – especially since the process of watching sixty shots a minute for more than forty-seven minutes is grueling by itself – but the laborious process has been willingly (if somewhat grudgingly) accepted. The experience of learning the correspondences is the central analogy of the second section. It replicates the experience of learning that set of terms and rules necessary for the exploration of any intellectual field. It is particularly reminiscent of the process of learning a foreign language – we must memorize what particular vocabulary words mean and how they fit into meaningful sequences – but it applies equally to mathematics and the sciences and to other areas of the arts and humanities. The overall change from thrilling rush to exhaustion and finally relief and sense of completion (once the final substitution is made and the section ends) is analogous to the experiences we have as we move into any new intellectual discipline and explore it in depth.

73

The overall change in the second section of *Zorns Lemma* from the focus on the alphabet to the focus on continuous activities suggests among other things the way in which we develop both intellectual facility and an ability to accomplish practical tasks. The fact that the environmental words are seen first, and the substitution imagery later, makes sense, since in most instances our ability to function practically in the world requires that we've learned to read and, in a more general sense, to be able to organize and internalize bits of information codified by words. Further, the segmenting of continuous activities into one-second bits replicates the one-step-at-a-time procedure we need to learn in order to complete practical or intellectual tasks: Frampton once said, "There are no complex ideas, only long series of simple ideas."[3]

A further dimension of the process of maturation is suggested by the fact that while many of the replacement activities are of finite duration, Frampton's arrangement of the individual segments of these activities toys with viewers' time sense. In real time, it takes the man who walks a city block – the replacement image for H – fifty-eight seconds to round the corner and disappear (or, really, fifty-six seconds, since in the final set of images he peeks back around the corner, surprising those viewers who have assumed his walk is candidly recorded, and revealing that he has walked for Frampton as Muybridge's subjects walked for him – acting out the appearance of candidness), but his walk takes more than twenty minutes in film time. On the other hand, Frampton begins to change a tire (T) during the eighty-second alphabetic set, and seems to complete the job in twenty-eight seconds, spread over approximately eleven minutes of film time. Other replacement images document portions of ongoing activities, and still others record cyclical natural phenomena that have no conclusion: ocean waves breaking (Z), a tree in winter (F). One of the challenges of the world that language delivers us into is coming to understand and learning to prioritize the network of patterns within patterns that creates the context for human experience. Our lives are inevitably part of different patterns simultaneously, and the best we can hope for is to maintain a healthy balance of these patterns as long as possible: Ideally our attempts to build a meaningful career on the basis of what we learn will be successful before we complete the inevitable physical process of birth, aging, and death.

Some years after completing *Zorns Lemma,* Frampton himself provided a reading of the film's second section:

Cortically speaking, we are of distinct and separate minds.... Generally, it would appear that, in right-handed persons, the left hemisphere is concerned with language and with linear and analytic language-like deductive activities. The right hemisphere is concerned generally with synthesizing nonlinear inductive activities.... My own reading of the forty-five-minute central section of *Zorns Lemma,* in which the image that is statistically before one passes gradually from a language-dominated one to a continuous non-language-dominated one, is a kind of allegory, an acting out of a transference of power from one hemisphere of the brain to the other. Of course, that was nowhere within my thinking of the film when I was making it.[4]

Whereas the second section of *Zorns Lemma* tends to create a sense of overload and exhaustion in the viewer, the final section comes as a relief. Even though the one-shot-per-second rhythm is maintained on the sound-track, the overall mood of the section is one of calm. Once again, the experience Frampton has created for the viewer is analogous to the stage of intellectual development the section focuses on: the achievement of philosophical/spiritual awareness and serenity. It is clear, well before the man, woman, and dog reach the distant woods, that this section will not end

A scarlet ibis, the final replacement image in the second section of *Zorns Lemma.*

until they have traversed the fields between the camera and the woods (the fact that so many of the activities in Section 2 are structured into the grid so as to become "clocks" for measuring our temporal position within the section has prepared us to make this deduction). There is nothing for the viewer's eye to do during the interim except explore the lovely winter scene and to notice how the sun's going behind intermittent clouds affects the look of the landscape. If the second section is extended climax, this section is an extended dénouement during which we get to see at least the illusion of the world as whole. The section's meditation on landscape is reminiscent of the belief, so prevalent during the nineteenth century, that contact with the spiritual dimension of existence or with God is available in nature. The subtle transformation of the scene by the intermittent sunlight is particularly suggestive of Luminist landscape painting, especially since the spiritual implications of light are directly spelled out in the text we are hearing as we watch the scene.[5]

Although on one level the soundtrack may seem rather out of sync with the visuals – the awkwardness in the reading created by having successive words spoken by different speakers is emphasized by the metronome sound – it is both philosophically and literally appropriate. In a philosophic sense, Grosseteste's treatise is an attempt to understand the entirety of the perceivable world as an emblem of the spiritual. And, on the literal level, what Grosseteste describes in the eleventh century is demonstrated by the twentieth-century film image: For a filmmaker, after all, light *is* the "first bodily form," which, literally, draws out "matter along with itself into a mass as great as the fabric of the world." When the six readers review the numbers from 1 to 10 (10 being "the full number of the universe"), it is difficult to ignore that the fence over which the walkers step halfway to the woods defines ten intervals from the left side of the film frame to the right. The film image thus becomes a metaphor for the universe; the filmmaker analogous to God; and the walkers analogous to the viewers whose trek from one end of the film to another is a cinematic emblem of our real lives.

The final moments of *Zorns Lemma* confirm this set of analogies. After the reading of the passage from Grosseteste is complete, the film continues for a minute or so more: The man, woman, and dog reach the distant woods and enter, and after a moment the screen flares to white. Given its position within the structure of *Zorns Lemma,* the moment when the walkers enter the woods is certainly suggestive of death – one is reminded of Robert Frost's "Stopping by Woods on a Snowy Evening." And the flare-out to white not only signals the end of the roll and the film, it is suggestive of the widespread observation by those who have had near-death experiences that, at the moment of death, we see a powerful light. Finally, since Frampton may have assumed that the coming of the light at the end of *Zorns Lemma* would be followed by the lights coming on in the theater and the audience filing out, the exit of the man, woman, and dog from the field is not only echoed by the viewers' exit from the cinematic incarnation, but is prescient of our ultimate exits from life, and the concluding moment of our intellectual growth.

In the years following the completion of *Zorns Lemma,* Frampton worked on two major film projects: *Hapax Legomena,* a seven-part film completed in 1972; and *Magellan,* a thirty-six-hour film meant to be seen calendrically over the course of 371 days, which was nearly complete when Frampton died in 1984. *Magellan* occupied Frampton for more than ten years. In fact, the idea for the epic was already germinating when he was shooting *Zorns Lemma:* In the replacement image for *A,* the book the hands are turning the pages of is Antonio Pigafetta's diary of his voyage with Magellan.[6] While *Zorns Lemma* uses the alphabet as an organizational grid, *Magellan* uses the calendar. Frampton made a film for each day of the year, and special films for special days: the solstices, the equinoxes. While I have seen most of *Magellan* (since titles of individual sections changed during the years when they were being shot, and individual films were periodically revised, it's difficult to be positive about how complete my viewing of the epic has been), I have not seen it presented as a yearly cycle. In fact, current institutions for film exhibition and distribution are ill-equipped for showing the film as Frampton presumably meant it to be seen. In this sense, *Magellan* offers a challenge to the current state of film accessibility, a challenge based on Frampton's admiration of epic literature, and particularly for Joyce's *Ulysses* and *Finnegan's Wake:* For Frampton the challenge was to extend cinematic horizons so that the pleasures and revelations of cinematic thought could be as flexible, in terms of accessibility, as the experience of reading serious literature.[7]

As interesting as Frampton's concept for *Magellan* is, I am not convinced that the concept is successfully fleshed out in the films that make it up, though there are remarkable moments, including *Gloria!* (1979), the film in which Frampton dedicates *Magellan* to his maternal grandmother. A set of poignant, witty computer-generated texts about his Irish grandmother is combined with two early commercial narratives about Irish wakes, and with a passage of lovely green film leader accompanied by a tune played on an Irish folk instrument described in one of the computer-generated texts. *Gloria!* is a film about death, about the spatial/temporal margins of experience and of cinema. In the final section of *Zorns Lemma,* Frampton looked

77

at "death" from a distance, as a metaphor. By the time he made *Gloria!*, he had experienced the deaths of his grandmother and father, and he knew he had cancer: His voyage "around the world" in *Magellan* (and around the two hemispheres of the brain) had brought him across that snowy field to the edge of the woods themselves.[8]

NOTES

1. Bruce Jenkins and Susan Krane's *Hollis Frampton, Recollections/Recreations* (Buffalo, NY and Cambridge, MA: Albright-Knox Art Gallery and MIT Press, 1984), a catalogue for a traveling exhibition of Frampton's nonfilm work that toured the United States in 1984–5, includes extensive information about, and illustration of, Frampton's photographic series, several of which refer to or are reminiscent of Muybridge. Frampton was to remain interested in making photographs and in writing about the history of photography throughout his career. His writings, including his interesting essay on Muybridge, "Eadweard Muybridge: Fragments of a Tesseract," are collected in *Circles of Confusion* (Rochester, NY: Visual Studies Workshop Press, 1983).
2. Frampton describes the burlesque in his comments on the now lost *A Running Man* (1963) in Scott MacDonald, *A Critical Cinema* (Berkeley, CA: University of California Press, 1988), pp. 26–7.
3. Frampton made this remarkable observation to me during informal conversation.
4. *A Critical Cinema*, pp. 58–9.
5. For a discussion of the Luminists, see Barbara Novak, *Nature and Culture* (New York: Oxford, 1980), pp. 28–33.
6. This is not evident in *Zorns Lemma*. Frampton indicates that it was Pigafetta's diary in *A Critical Cinema*, p. 51.
7. I have always had a suspicion that Frampton used Joyce's literary career as a model for his own career as filmmaker. Joyce began with short stories; Frampton, with short films. *Zorns Lemma* is Frampton's *Portrait of an Artist as a Young Man; Hapax Legomena*, his *Ulysses; Magellan*, his *Finnegan's Wake*. There is no point in trying to elaborate this parallel in a note, but I am confident that it is not only generally suggestive, but can be developed in some detail, work by work.
8. The two most useful sources of information about Frampton's life are Susan Krane's "Chronology" in *Hollis Frampton, Recollections/Recreations*, and Barry Goldensohn's "Memoir of Hollis Frampton" in the special Frampton issue of *October*, no. 32 (Spring 1985), pp. 7–16.

7
Laura Mulvey and
Peter Wollen
Riddles of the Sphinx

Although Frampton's films often critique the narrow scope of intellect ministered to by the conventional narrative cinema, by generating film experiences that require viewers to think more energetically than is customary in movie theaters, his critique is limited by its generality. Frampton explored many elements of film history and film practice, but he seems to have assumed that, basically – *intellectually* – a film viewer is a film viewer, and that the expectations created in audiences by a history of seeing conventional movies are largely consistent from one viewer to another. By the mid-1970s, however, in Europe and in North America, film theorists were involved in what has become a sustained investigation of the implications of the gendering of film history. It has become increasingly clear that to question cinematic conventions is to question the ways in which cultural assumptions about the meaning of gender are embedded within film experiences. Some of the most innovative work in this area has been done by Laura Mulvey and Peter Wollen, both in their theoretical writings and, more importantly for our purposes here, in the films they have collaborated on, the most influential of which is *Riddles of the Sphinx*.

For both Mulvey and Wollen, the making of films has functioned as a means of demonstrating and elaborating speculations they have explored in written texts. Wollen is a distinguished film theorist; his *Signs and Meaning in the Cinema* (London and Bloomington: Indiana University Press, 1969) was an influential early introduction to a broader range of film-theoretical concerns; his "Two Avant-Gardes" brought widespread recognition to the fact that, by the 1970s, filmmakers disenchanted with the conventional cinema had developed at least two major schools of critical filmmaking.[1] One of these, an esthetically radical school, is identified with the Cooperative movement in North America and Europe and is epitomized

by the filmmakers in Part 1 of this volume. This school has its roots in the French and German avant-garde films of the 1920s; it is powerfully influenced by the fine arts. The second avant-garde is epitomized by Jean-Luc Godard, Miklos Jansco, Jean-Marie Straub and Daniele Huillet, and others whose experimental narratives critique industry narrative codes. This approach has its roots in the revolutionary Soviet films of the 1920s. For Wollen, the real issue was not which of the two avant-gardes was more esthetically or politically correct; it was how to bring these two alternative cinemas together to mount a more exhaustive and effective critique of commercial cinema. After all, both avant-gardes function in opposition to conventional movie-making.

Laura Mulvey's "Visual Pleasure and Narrative Cinema" (originally published in *Screen* in Autumn 1975) is probably the single most influential (and most frequently anthologized) theoretical article of the past twenty-five years: Its analysis of the "male gaze" as a crucial convention of mainstream cinema history has generated extensive debate and has inspired a good many filmmakers. Mulvey's essay has a precise goal:

> It is said that analyzing pleasure, or beauty, destroys it. That is the intention of this article. The satisfaction and reinforcement of the ego that represent the high point of film history hitherto must be attacked. Not in favor of a reconstructed new pleasure, which cannot exist in the abstract, nor of intellectualized unpleasure, but to make way for a total negation of the ease and plenitude of the narrative fiction film. The alternative is the thrill that comes from leaving the past behind without rejecting it, transcending outworn or oppressive forms, or daring to break with normal pleasurable expectations in order to conceive a new language of desire.[2]

As Mulvey indicates, it is not enough to state one's opposition to conventional cinema and its mechanisms for catering to a particular definition of male desire; rather, a new progressive cinema must be developed so that the conventions of mainstream film history can be subverted within the theater, and a new audience, with new filmic assumptions and expectations, can be discovered.

Penthesilea (1974) and *Riddles of the Sphinx* were developed as instances of a progressive new cinema. Indeed, the very fact that both were the result

---

From Shots 1, 3, and 9 of "Louise's story told in thirteen shots," from Laura Mulvey and Peter Wollen's *Riddles of the Sphinx* (1977). Courtesy British Film Institute.

of an equal collaboration between a man and a woman was a response to the male-dominated, hierarchical production process standard in the industry. *Penthesilea* explores the myth of the Amazon, using formal tactics familiar from European and North American avant-garde film.[3] Because it has not been generally available for years, *Penthesilea* has had only marginal influence. *Riddles of the Sphinx,* on the other hand, has become one of the most widely discussed critical films of recent decades.[4]

Like *Zorns Lemma, Riddles of the Sphinx* has a precise formal organization. Unlike Frampton, however, Mulvey and Wollen make their general structure evident from the opening moments. After the title and a brief quote from Gertrude Stein's *How to Write* – "A narrative of what wishes what it wishes it to be" – we are presented with an outline of the film's seven-part organization:

1. Opening pages
2. Laura speaking
3. Stones
4. Louise's story told in thirteen shots
5. Acrobats
6. Laura listening
7. Puzzle ending[5]

The seven named sections are more than sequentially arranged. As the film proceeds, we realize that the first three sections are roughly mirrored by the final three. The "Opening pages" section reveals hands turning the pages of a book of traditional mythic images of women as seen by men: a witch on a broom, harpies, a spider woman, a mermaid – ending with an image of the Egyptian sphinx with Greta Garbo's face. Essentially, this history of imaging women as mysterious, dangerous beings is a puzzle, a labyrinthine riddle, that Mulvey/Wollen mean to explore. And this puzzle beginning is mirrored by the seventh section, during which we see hands manipulating a small plastic labyrinth game, the object of which is to maneuver two drops of mercury into the center: The hands are successful in getting the mercury into the center of the puzzle. Both the opening section and the final section are one shot long (one minute, five seconds, and three minutes, respectively).

The second section intercuts between shots of imagery of the Egyptian and Greek sphinxes, and of Mulvey, seen in medium shot, sitting at a table on which are a coffee cup (a map of the world is printed on it), a pencil sharpener in the shape of a globe, and a microphone and tape recorder. This 3½-minute passage is organized so that while at first we are seeing the sphinx imagery and hearing Mulvey, the shots of Mulvey get longer. Mulvey explains that when she and Wollen "were planning the central section of the film, about a mother and child, we decided to use the voice of the sphinx as an imaginary narrator – because the sphinx represents, not the voice of truth, not an answering voice, but its opposite: a questioning voice, a voice asking a riddle. The Oedipus myth associates the voice of the sphinx with motherhood as mystery and with resistance to patriarchy." During the remainder of her brief reading, Mulvey traces the history of the sphinx from her life outside the gate of the city in the Oedipus story to the revival of the Egyptian sphinx after Napoleon's campaigns in Egypt: the Egyptian sphinx is male but his blank face has traditionally been a site onto which men have projected their fears and fantasies about women. "Laura speaking" is mirrored by "Laura listening," a slightly shorter passage during which we watch Mulvey sitting at the same table, listening to a tape recording of herself.

The third section, "Stones," is a montage of found footage of the Egyptian sphinx, rephotographed, as Mulvey and Wollen were to indicate later, "through a number of generations with the aid of a motion-analyser projector, using zooms, step motion, slow and reverse motion, freeze frames, and extreme close-up (concentrating on the sphinx's mouth) eventually showing film grain"; this seven-minute, fourteen-second passage is mirrored by "Acrobats," a six-minute, forty-four-second passage during which imagery of women acrobats – a tumbler, a juggler, a trapeze artist – is optically printed in both black and white and gorgeous color.

Altogether the mirrored pairs of sections create a visual and conceptual frame around the long (fifty-four minutes, nine seconds) fourth section, "Louise's story told in thirteen shots," and to some extent function as a set of "befores" and "afters." The procedures used in the framing sections are often reminiscent of procedures explored in the late 1960s and early 1970s by filmmakers identified by Wollen as part of the esthetic avant-garde ("Stones" has a lot in common, for example, with Ken Jacobs's *Tom, Tom, the Piper's Son (1969–71);* and Mulvey's recording herself and listening to the recording recalls Morgan Fisher's *Documentary Footage*), while the central section is, at least in a general sense, reminiscent of the commercial cinema: Louise's story is a melodrama in which characters (played by actors) enact a continuous story. In this sense, the mirrored pairs of framing sections separate and encapsulate the more conventional melodrama – or serve as a margin (spatial/temporal, conceptual, esthetic) around the narrative – so that by the time viewers reach the story and after it seems complete, they know it is part of a larger set of filmic issues and options.

Although the central section of *Riddles of the Sphinx* is more conventional

83

than the framing passages, its highly unusual formal strategies align it with the experimental narratives by Godard, Daniele Huillet and Jean-Marie Straub, and other directors who developed critiques of mainstream cinema from more fully within the commercial arena, that is, with what Wollen called the political avant-garde. As the title indicates, "Louise's story" is made up of thirteen continuous shots (the shortest is one minute, forty-two seconds; the longest, ten minutes, eight seconds), which, taken together, form a grid that dramatizes the developing independence of a woman, Louise (Dinah Stabb), and her step-by-step movement from inside the home, where she is a wife and mother, out of her marriage and into the working world, toward an increasing awareness of the sociopolitical status of women and the possibility of taking action to improve her (and her daughter's) personal situation and the future for women in general. Each of these thirteen shots takes the form of a continuous $360°$ pan, and each is separated from the next by a twelve-second passage of text. While each pan encapsulates a stage of the larger ongoing process of Louise's development within a camera gesture that clearly has a beginning and end, the intertexts are fragmentary (the first, for instance, is "Perhaps Louise is too close to her child. How much longer can she reject the outside world, other people, other demands. Her husband often"), though each provides a relevant introduction for the shot that follows. The $360°$ pans are slow and regular, and often survey a limited space – Louise's small kitchen in the first shot, for example. Not only do these stately camera movements give each shot/scene a formal structure, they implicitly critique conventional camerawork.

In conventional movies the moving camera usually works in one of two ways: Either a scene is defined by the film frame and the camera tracks or zooms into this space toward a particular element of the framed space (a method employed also by *Wavelength* and *Serene Velocity*), or the camera pans or tracks across an implicitly larger fictional or documentary space toward a particular element of the larger scene that relates to the narrative (or sometimes merely to express the expanse of the particular space within which the narrative is developing). These movements toward preconceived goals usually function as elements in the larger, equally goal-oriented thrusts of cinematic narratives, and these narratives, in turn, move relentlessly toward the reconfirmation of what has been a largely patriarchal industry within a largely patriarchal society. In this sense, the forwardness of conventional camerawork can be seen as implicitly phallic.

The camera movements in the thirteen shots that tell Louise's story are precisely the opposite. Whereas conventional camera movements tend to penetrate into the field of vision defined by the frame, the movements to

84

the right or left in *Riddles of the Sphinx* relentlessly explore the margins and continually redefine whatever is seen in the center of the frame by expanding, rather than narrowing its context. In fact, the convention of centering characters within the frame is subverted in these 360° pans: Characters walk through the frame or the frame moves past them.

The general implications of the 360° pans are extensively elaborated by the visual worlds the individual pans reveal. For many first-time viewers who bring conventional expectations into a screening of *Riddles of the Sphinx,* "Louise's story told in thirteen shots" seems empty of action: The slow pace of the pans and the rigorous grid the pans create tend to thwart conventional viewer excitement. But, in fact, the mise-en-scène of each of the thirteen shots is densely suggestive. For all practical purposes, each pan is a minifilm revealing a particular location crucial to Louise's developing consciousness.

In the first shot we see Louise working in her kitchen, holding her daughter (the daughter and the mother's torso are the focus of the camera; we never see Louise's face in this shot), and making a scrambled egg for the child. The camera turns as Louise moves around her carefully arranged kitchen; the circularity of the pan is confirmed by circular and semicircular objects within the image – dishes, fruit, the eggs, the way Louise turns a piece of toast to cut off the crust – and by both the music and the poetic narration on the soundtrack: Mike Ratledge's music is repetitive and serial (in a manner generally reminiscent of Philip Glass, Terry Reilly, and Steve Reich), as is the narration, which uses a repeated rhythm and repeated phrases – "Time to get ready. Time to come in. Things to forget. Things to lose. Meal time. Story time.... " Both music and narration suggest Louise's immersion in her intimacy with Anna; the narration is an internal monologue during which Louise, essentially, talks to herself. Altogether the passage creates a sense of the relentless, engrossing round of caring for a small child – a subject absolutely outside the purview of most conventional cinema, where any sustained attention to the "trivialities" of domestic labor and its political implications is rigorously avoided, except for purposes of humor.

The conclusion of the shot suggests an ending to the particular stage in Louise's development. Just as the camera reaches the space where the shot began, a man's hand intrudes into the image from the right and takes a piece of the toast. As the man's arm is subsequently revealed, we see, under his arm, a newspaper with the words, "home" and "mortgage" headlined. The intrusion has multilevel implications. That it is felt by Louise to be an unpleasant interruption of her engrossing intimacy with her daughter is suggested by the fact that the man's brown sport coat clashes with the blue of Louise's clothes and of the decor. Further, the fact of the newspaper, with its suggestions of the larger world and of the traditional male role as breadwinner, mortgage payer, suggests that Louise's personal discomfort with Chris's presence here is an instance of the much more general problem of the constricting, exploitative organization of gender roles within the conventional family structure. On the level of the *child*'s developing awareness, the arrival of the father with his newspaper is a visualization of the Lacanian insight into the importance of language in the formation of the child's subconscious: The oppression of women is reconfirmed by the child's learning language which, in its current evolution, is inevitably the language of patriarchy.

The remaining twelve shots that make up Louise's story chart her journey out into the larger world. The grid of continuous 360° pans is organized into four triads divided by a pivotal seventh shot. During the first triad, we see Louise in the home, "protected" from the outside world as a child is in the womb, though it is clear from the intrusion of the man's hand at the end of the first shot that her "safety" in this womblike state is compromised and temporary. During the second pan, Louise and her daughter are in the child's room at bedtime; and finally, in the third, watch as Chris finishes moving out of the house. This third shot is the first view outside, though at this point Louise (and the viewer) remains inside: Chris is seen through the windows and front door.

During the second triad, Louise leaves the home and begins to confront the realities of the outside world: In the fourth shot she leaves Anna at a day-care center; in the fifth, we see her working as a telephone operator; and in the sixth, she goes to the lunchroom, where she and her co-workers discuss the problems of child care. The second triad of shots is distinguished from the first not only by the fact that the three locations are all outside the home, but by a fundamental change in the soundtrack: The music and narration used in the first three shots is replaced, in the second triad, by sync-sound conversations between Louise and other women. Further, the mise-en-scène of the fourth through sixth shots confirms Louise's journey outward: At the day-care center, Anna meets other children and Louise talks with Maxine; as a telephone operator she connects people in different parts of the outside world with each other – a function emphasized by a large map of the world mounted on a wall where the telephone operators work and the colorful travel posters that decorate the walls of the lunchroom. Of course, the world into which Louise journeys is controlled by men; women are limited to service roles.

The seventh shot is pivotal on several levels. The fact that this shot is precisely at the center of the film assures its importance, as does the fact that it is the only shot in Louise's story during which the camera not only pans, but moves on its base: The camera travels around a traffic circle as it pans, finally pulling even with a van inside which several women (including Louise) are talking; ultimately the van and the camera diverge. Viewers find themselves "in motion" in a new sense, and the disconcerting movement helps express the importance of what actually occurs in the shot: The women are discussing the possibility of working together to force the union to consider child care on the job as a part of reasonable working conditions. The women's collaborating to make changes in the structures of patriarchy offers the possibility of altering the foundations on which patriarchy rests, and to alter these foundations is to begin a process that will affect not only child care and telephone service but all contemporary institutions, including cinematic ones. The fact that the shot is inventively conceived and technically brilliant confirms Mulvey and Wollen's excitement about these new, progressive possibilities. Indeed, if we accept Mulvey's frequent description of the film's structure as a pyramid, the seventh shot is the pyramid's pinnacle.

In the third triad we return to the domestic arena, but in a different way.

From Shot 12 of "Louise's story told in thirteen shots," from *Riddles of the Sphinx*. Courtesy British Film Institute.

Here, Louise is not alone with Anna, isolated from both the outside, patriarchal world and other women. In the eighth shot Louise is seen with Anna and Maxine at a shopping center crowded with women; in the ninth shot she is with Anna at a playground (other women and children are there as well), thinking about working conditions: She has lost her job, but her working experience has raised a set of questions that lead "both out into society and back into her own memory. Future and past seemed to be locked together. She felt a gathering of strength but no certainty of success"; in the tenth shot Louise and Maxine visit Louise's mother who is now caring for Anna: The mother and Anna work in the garden while Louise and Maxine sort through old family photographs.

The final triad charts the final stages of Louise's development, stages that reveal a new confidence. During the first half of her story, Louise is either hidden away at home or insecure about her situation outside the home: Her anxieties about Anna and about her relationship with Anna are clear at the day-care center, at the phone company, and even during the discussion at the roundabout, where Louise's participation in the conversation is primarily in the form of questions. On one level, Louise's journey only takes her from one patriarchal site to another; and Mulvey/Wollen's arrangement of the thirteen shots of her story as a series of mirror reflections emphasizes this: The 360° pans are arranged around the pivotal seventh pan in "mirroring" pairs. In Shot 1, Louise is enclosed, almost entombed, in her domestic existence; in Shot 13, she visits a museum where bodies of mummies are enclosed within coffins within glass cases within rooms of the museum. In Shot 2, she visits her daughter's bedroom; in Shot 12, she is with Maxine in her (their) bedroom. In Shot 3, Chris leaves the home; in Shot 11, she visits his workplace. And so on. Nevertheless, though Louise is always seen as a captive of patriarchy, the final three shots of her story reveal her becoming more active on her own behalf, seeking out a more complex understanding of women's experience.

In the eleventh shot, when Louise and Maxine visit Chris at his film/video studio, he wants to show them footage he is working on, of Mary Kelly discussing her 1976 *Post Partum Document* (the work is about that stage of Kelly's relationship with her young son during which the child begins nursery school). Louise wants to tell Chris that she has decided to sell the house: It may be, as he says, "a bad time to sell," but, Louise explains, "It's a good time for *me* to sell." The fact that Louise has made a decision about an important financial issue (an issue that earlier in her story seemed the terrain of men) is evidence of her developing independence and clarity about herself. The importance of this new assurance is expressed formally by the fact that this 360° pan moves to the left, not to the right as all the previous pans do: Psychologically and cinematically, Louise is moving in a different direction, a direction that is confirmed in the final two pans.

In the twelfth shot, in Maxine's elaborately decorated apartment, Louise is reading aloud the text of a complex dream Maxine has recorded. As Louise's reading reveals the intricacies of the dream, the complex ways in which it reflects/distorts reality, the left-panning camera throws the viewer into a visual labyrinth where perspective is confused by many mirrors. In a growing child, the mirror stage corresponds to the development of a sense of individuality, which is achieved through the child's separation from the mother by means of the intercession of the father and the outside world he represents. As is clear in Louise's story (and in the passage from Kelly's *Post Partum Document*), the child's achievement of separation from the mother is inevitably accompanied by the mother's separation from the child; and both members of what has previously been a dyad must come to grips with their own individuality, their own independence. For Louise the process must take a different form than it does for Anna. When the child is first seeing herself in the mirror, she is seeing herself complete for the first time: The image looks more complete than the child may feel. As an adult, Louise must contend not simply with her image, but with the ways in which women's self-imagery has been distorted by patriarchal society: What women see in the mirror is largely determined by how men have demanded women to be seen and to see themselves. This is emphasized near the end of the twelfth shot when – in one of the film's most stunning moments – the camera pans past a mirror that reveals the camera itself and the woman (cinematographer Diane Tammes) turning the handle that causes the camera to pan. Conventional film has been one of the primary means (or "mirrors") by which patriarchy has revealed how women should look and act, and the sudden gap in the illusion of the twelfth shot, revealing the camera being operated by a woman, not only communicates Louise's need to see past conventional illusions about women, but the commitment of Wollen and Mulvey to redressing, in film, some of the distortions of conventional film history.

For Louise, the achievement of a new sense of self is a challenge that requires sustained questioning and, as is evident in the final shot of her story, research: Louise and Anna walk through the Egyptian Room of the British Museum (no longer as a dyad: Anna is no longer carried; she walks beside her mother), presumably exploring the mythic history of women, as we hear music and a voice-over reviewing a symbolic dream (or telling a poetic story) about "her" childhood and a passage from a book "she"

89

remembers having read somewhere in which a woman opens a box labeled "Anatomy is no longer destiny," and discovers a Greek sphinx that repeats three words: "Capital," "Delay," and "Body." At first, we may assume that the ambiguous "she" and "her" refer to Louise, but when we look closely at the story itself, it seems to be Anna's story or, perhaps, Louise's imagining of what Anna may remember at a later date. If indeed the "she" of the final pan is Anna, Louise's story ends, not simply with her redefinition of herself in relation to patriarchy, but with the implication that Louise's actions will have helped to free Anna.

The changes we see in Louise between the first and last shots of her story are confirmed by the differences between the first three sections of the film and their "mirror reflections" in the final three sections. Just after Anna imagines flinging herself through the air in her apparent joy of having learned to listen to the voice of the sphinx (the feminine) inside herself, Louise's story ends and the optically printed passage of the three acrobats begins. This passage and the one that mirrors it – "Stones" – are about "projection," but in two different senses. As we watch the increasingly abstract images of the face of the sphinx in "Stones," we tend to "see" imagery; we project faces onto the stones, the way we project images onto cloud formations as children, and the way men have traditionally projected their own fantasies onto the physical reality of women. In "Acrobats," however, the projection is physical – three women "project" their own bodies, controlling their actions in defiance of gravity – but representative also of psychic freedom, the ability to project one's mind wherever one wants. Laura's listening to herself in the following section confirms the idea of listening to the voice of the woman within oneself, and thus represents an advance over Laura's review of the history of the marginalization of womanness in "Laura Speaking" – though, of course, she must have first recognized the realities of this history before she can move on from it. And finally, completing the maze puzzle, which requires persistence and balance, represents an improvement over being defined and represented *as* a puzzle – as women are in the images revealed in "Opening pages" (that *two* drops of mercury are guided to the center of the maze suggests that Louise's development implies Anna's development).

In general, *Riddles of the Sphinx* explores forms of psychic development marginalized and/or elided by conventional movies. We travel *from* the point at which a woman has come to realize the degree to which her history has been co-opted by the projections of patriarchy *to* the point when she is acting on her own both to retrieve her suppressed past and to generate a new, progressive present and future. The kinds of changes that take place in Louise, and the various activities we see her engaged in, are a survey of subject matters the conventional cinema has ignored, on the grounds that moviegoers are not interested in domestic labor, the nurturing of children, day care, "women's" service occupations, friendship between women, friendship as an exploration of intellectual and political issues. . . .

And the mirror organization of the completed film, along with the film's other formal devices – the grid of continuous circular pans during Louise's story, the use of printed intertitles between the pans, the avant-garde procedures used in the triad of opening and closing passages – defies the rules of conventional story development. There *is* a story but it is presented with procedures that, in conventional terms, detract from the story's velocity, and draw attention to the process of filmmaking itself. Whereas conventional film tends to mirror the patriarchal structures of society, *Riddles of the Sphinx* holds a mirror up to conventional film, revealing its limitations and distortions. By means of its structure, the Mulvey/Wollen film redefines the position of the audience: Instead of using the film experience as a way of complacently gazing through a male "window onto reality," viewers of the Mulvey/Wollen film are looking at a film that reflects on conventional cinematic topics and procedures. Or, to return to the Gertrude Stein line with which the film begins, *Riddles of the Sphinx* is a narrative of what wishes (the film is a wish in the direction of a new cinema) what it (this film) wishes it (Film) to be. The story within the film about Louise, Anna, Chris, and Maxine is part of the larger narrative that includes the making of the film (our seeing the camera person during the twelfth shot makes clear that the fiction we've been watching is a part of a larger, real process that has presumably grown out of struggles by other women, including Mulvey, similar to those Louise is experiencing), and the viewer's struggles in coming to understand the structure and implications of *Riddles of the Sphinx*.

The experience of watching *Zorns Lemma* demands considerable energy, and, in particular, types of intellectual energy avoided by the conventional cinema. In *Riddles of the Sphinx*, Mulvey and Wollen go a step further. As unconventional as the structure of *Zorns Lemma* is, viewers almost inevitably understand what that structure is, once they have experienced the film: In a sense, they are *carried into* the experience of memorizing the substitution images, in much the same way viewers of conventional films are carried into narrative. More is required of Mulvey/Wollen viewers. *Riddles of the Sphinx* uses so many kinds of information in a structure with so many individual parts that, especially on first viewing, the film itself seems a maze, its structure a riddle. The fact that *Riddles of the Sphinx* opens with an outline of the film's seven sections alerts viewers that *this* film – like a complex written essay – needs to be studied, not merely experienced. Further, the filmmakers make clear that they're involved in a cinematic investigation that predates this film and will continue after it, hopefully for the viewer, as well as for the filmmakers. The excerpt of Mary Kelly's *Post Partum Document* read during Louise's visit to Chris's editing room is implicitly a plea for further exploration on the part of viewers who may not be familiar with Kelly's work: A complete understanding of Mulvey/Wollen's use of the excerpt requires a more thorough examination of the Kelly text. Much the same implications are created in Mulvey's review of the history of the sphinx. *Riddles of the Sphinx* asks that we join the filmmakers and others as they attempt to have an ongoing progressive impact on one of the problematic psychosocial foundations of modern life and conventional cinema.

NOTES

1. "The Two Avant-Gardes" and other Wollen essays are collected in *Readings and Writings* (London: Verso Press, 1982).
2. "Visual Pleasure and Narrative Cinema" and other Mulvey essays are collected in *Visual and Other Pleasures* (Bloomington, IN: Indiana University Press, 1989).
3. *Penthesilea* is described in detail in *Screen*, vol. 15, no. 3 (1974), p. 120. See also E. Ann Kaplan's comments on the film in *Women and Film* (New York: Methuen, 1983), pp. 162–63.
4. For a review of this discussion, and an extended analysis of the film's exploration of the relation of the sphinx myths and the issue of gender, see Lucy Fischer, *Shot/Countershot* (Princeton, NJ: Princeton University Press, 1989), Chapter 2.
5. The complete text of *Riddles of the Sphinx* was published in *Screen*, vol. 18, no. 2 (Summer 1977), pp. 61–77.

8
James Benning
American Dreams

The Frampton and Mulvey/Wollen films focused on in Chapters 6 and 7 critique general intellectual limitations of conventional cinema by developing structures that are radically different from the structures of mass-market movies. In the experimental narratives that established his reputation – *8½ × 11* (1974) and *11 × 14* (1976) – James Benning takes a different tack: He uses a good many of the conventional gestures, but as points of departure in films that, ultimately, surprise the very expectations they invoke. In his later films – and, in particular, in *American Dreams* – he goes a step further: He invokes and critiques his own practice as critical film-maker, laying bare his complicity with attitudes about gender that are embedded in both conventional and critical cinema.

8½ × 11 is made up of twenty-eight one-shot vignettes, intercut so as to highlight two stories: Two women drive along interstate highways, pick up two young hitchhikers, go to a motel with them to have sex, drop them off and continue their trip; a farm worker hitchhikes to a job, works, rests, then hitchhikes on. The two stories intersect only once, in the final shot, when the farm worker takes a bath in a stream underneath an overpass we see the women's car cross. In conventional films, we are usually quite clear about the progress of a narrative; if there is a particular gap or ambiguity, it's the mystery that needs to be solved: Inevitably, when the film is over, we recognize that every incident, every shot is part of a single coherent (or at least "coherent") whole in which all characters have specific, definable relationships to one another, and each of their actions has a clear causal relationship to the plot. In *8½ × 11*, viewers must continually search for the narrative. The irony is that once it is constructed, and its particular coherence evident, the film's cinematic unconventionality is all the more apparent: *These* characters have absolutely no connection to one another

93

other than the fact that in one instance they physically cross paths and share the same general geographic space for a single moment.[1] In $8\frac{1}{2} \times 11$ the characters' journey through the American landscape is the viewer's journey out of conventional film expectations.

Generally in his early films, Benning focuses on American landscapes and cityscapes, composing images so that events move through the frame, often in ways that draw attention not only to the presence of the camera, but to viewers' assumptions about what can happen in a shot. In one shot in 11×14, for example, a tractor is pulling a haywagon across a field in the general direction of the camera but toward the right of the frame; when the tractor moves off screen to the right, we assume the shot is over, and are surprised when, a moment later, the tractor crosses from right to left in the near foreground, and then, after leaving the image again, moves from the left side of the image away from the camera into the distance. From our conventional moviegoing, we have assumed that motion within a shot is primarily relevant to the development of narrative action, but here Benning's choreography of the shot becomes an end in itself that does touch on the narrative of a farm worker whose travels we've been following – he is seen on the back of the thresher as it passes in front of the camera – but only as a pretext for Benning's formal gesture.

American Dreams represents, on one hand, a complete break from Benning's earlier interest in the American landscape and cityscape and the formal means Benning had developed for depicting the world, and, on the other hand, an important extension of his concern with using filmmaking as critique. For fifty-eight minutes the viewer sees only baseball cards and other memorabilia relating to the career of Hank Aaron, and various printed and written texts, accompanied by a soundtrack made up of regularly alternating phrases of popular songs of the period from 1954 through 1976 and moments from famous speeches of the same years. The Aaron memorabilia is presented chronologically, so that viewers can trace the development of this remarkable career and its supreme achievement: Aaron's passing Babe Ruth's all-time home-run total. Regular superimposed numbers reveal the total home runs Aaron had hit by the end of each year, and the soundtrack concludes with a recording of a radio announcer's call of the home run that set a new record.

Aaron's achievement of his American dream occurs within a context of other American "dreams," of a variety of kinds, created by the excerpts

---

Three images from James Benning's *American Dreams* (1984).

95

from the songs and speeches included on the soundtrack. There are objects of romantic interest (in, for example, Roy Orbison's "Blue Angel" and Wayne Newton's "Red Roses for a Blue Lady"), political hopes or fantasies (in Barry Sadler's "The Ballad of the Green Berets" and Crosby, Stills, Nash, and Young's "Woodstock"). We are reminded of Senator Joseph McCarthy's fantasies of finding communists and avoiding exposure of his methods, of Kennedy and Nixon's dreams of becoming president (an excerpt from the Nixon–Kennedy debate is included), of Neil Armstrong's landing on the moon (a dream-come-true), of Angela Davis's dream of full equality for women.... These varied American dreams (and nightmares) are further contextualized by one other strand of information. Indeed, along with the Aaron memorabilia, it's the most crucial element in the film.

Despite his decision not to use actors or sets/locations in *American Dreams*, Benning does develop a character and a plot that provide a variety of references to conventional film melodrama. This character is the narrator of a rolling text that moves across the lower portion of the image from right to left for fifty-seven of the film's fifty-eight minutes. The author of this narrative is not identified until the conclusion of the film, and most viewers read it without knowing its source. Our discovery of who this narrator is becomes the lynchpin of Benning's critique.

Although *American Dreams* is serially organized (the only irregularities in the entire film are flashing texts that call attention to particularities in the Aaron memorabilia) and relatively minimal (except for the rolling text, there is no moving imagery at all), most viewers find the experience of the film quite demanding. The rolling text moves just quickly enough so that if viewers look away to examine another sector of the frame, they risk missing a detail of the narrative this text is developing. The fact that, early in the film, the narrator of the rolling text describes certain sexual adventures makes viewer attention to this strand of information almost inevitable. On the other hand, the regular changes in the memorabilia and the other textual information consistently tempt the viewer's eye and mind. As minimal as Benning's methods may first seem, they break with convention not only by virtue of the kinds of imagery Benning provides, but by giving viewers more information than they can comfortably take in. On one level, the resulting experience mirrors the experience of living through any historical period: We rarely feel we have a firm handle on the events happening around us. Indeed, our love of conventional film has a lot to do with our desire for a simple, coherent understanding of our experience and its relation to history.

Since the rolling text is not identified at the beginning, since it is a first-person narrative, and since it is handwritten, viewers often tend to identify with the narrator as a character, the way they have learned to identify with the detective–narrator in *cinéma noir*. Of course, many people see *American Dreams* in situations where it is presented as an avant-garde film and, in some cases, where Benning is present at the screening. In these instances, there is a tendency for viewers to assume that the diary we are reading is the filmmaker's – especially if they are aware that avant-garde filmmakers have often used filmmaking as a means of personal revelation. In Benning's case, such an identification is particularly appropriate: His interest in the diarist was partly a function of the fact that both men are natives of working-class neighborhoods in Milwaukee (where Aaron spent most of his baseball career), who were affected by many of the same events and issues. Regardless of whether we assume that the "I" is a character or the persona of the filmmaker, however, our tendency is to see the events the narrator describes from his point of view and, in some measure, to empathize with him. That this narrator's perspective on events is stereotypically male only confirms this process, since most of us, women and men, have been trained by conventional cinema to see as males.

As mentioned earlier, the opening passages of the narrator's diary raise the issue of sexuality. The narrator has apparently just left home to come to New York City for the first time. He is staying at a Howard Johnson's motel in Queens: "Downtown is barely visable with binoccular" (throughout his diary, the narrator misspells words, frequently creating inadvertent humor). On his first night at the motel, the narrator sees a beautiful naked lady through the curtains of a room across the way: "I had to watch her ...a thin vail of curtain allowed me to watch as she passionately kissed a man who wore cloths." The viewer becomes a voyeur of both the activities the narrator describes and of the narrator's own voyeurism – though it does become clear later that this diary is being written on the assumption that others will read it ("This will be one of the most closely read pages since the SCROLLS in those caves" [the Dead Sea Scrolls]). Several days later, he decides to go to a massage parlor where he picks out "the blond (the best looking I thought)," who leads him to a room, where she massages and finally tries to masturbate him, though the narrator finds he is uncomfortable with the situation: "She was here only for the money & knew she could make more by fucking but wouldn't. Whenever she was close I held her more private parts and she did not protest. I felt sorry for the kid. She was just like everybody else. It was a job & she was only in it for the money. I sat up for the last time, I'm sorry. She smiled. I said, O.K.?" Because of the narrator's feeling for the woman, it is difficult not to feel something for him: His attitudes and responses are certainly *male,* but they are understandable, even poignant – and quite conventional; Hollywood film history is full of instances where male protagonists develop sympathy for the prostitutes who service them.

As the narrator's story continues, viewer identification with him evolves. For a time viewers continue to understand him as a man not altogether unlike them (if they're men) or men they have known. But when they realize that the guns he is carrying are not those of a detective or an adolescent trying to act macho, that the narrator thinks about using these guns to assassinate President Richard Nixon, their attitude begins to change. Of course, even the idea of assassinating Nixon doesn't separate the narrator from all viewers: Many people, at one time or another, have fantasized about killing a head of state. But when it is clear that the narrator is pursuing Nixon and positioning himself to shoot him, viewers are forced to face the fact that this person they've been sharing the male gaze with, *identifying* with, is dangerous. The narrator journeys from state to state, even crossing the Canadian border at one point, following Nixon. After getting close to the president, but failing to shoot him, the narrator changes his target, revealing that his goal is not to kill Nixon in particular, just someone famous enough to make an assassin famous. Near the end of *American Dreams,* the narrator begins to follow George Wallace. At the end of the film's fifty-seventh minute, a single gunshot on the soundtrack is followed by Benning's identification of the narrator as Arthur Bremer, the man who wounded Wallace in Laurel, Maryland, on May 15, 1972.

By creating what seems to be a conventional sort of viewer–character identification and then revealing, first, that viewers should be rather uncomfortable with the identification they've established, and second, that what they've assumed is a fictional narration is relatively famous historically, Benning forces them to consider some of the implications of being a "normal" male in the United States and some of the limitations in our historical awareness of the world; that is, Benning uses the conventional process of identification to engage viewers with the film, then turns it against them, to reveal important dimensions of what conventional viewership *means.*

Although *American Dreams* creates a filmic journey through a period of recent American history, reminding viewers of crucial events and the dreams they embodied, and, in general, critiquing conventional narrative, it also provides a critique of American machismo that includes certain approaches to critical filmmaking. This critique is embodied most obviously in the film's central visual/conceptual juxtaposition: the career of Hank Aaron, as represented in the memorabilia (and at times on the soundtrack) and Arthur Bremer's experiences as a would-be assassin, as revealed in the rolling text (and by the gunshot and Benning's identification of the diary). On one level, Aaron's successful pursuit of Ruth's record is the precise opposite of Bremer's partially "successful" attempt to kill a political figure: Aaron's achievement is the quintessential American success story, and a heartening demonstration of the poverty of those racial assumptions that had kept African Americans out of the major leagues. Bremer's crime is a quintessential American nightmare. But on another level, the two narratives contain a significant parallel: Both reveal American males relentlessly, even obsessively, pursuing goals that, in the end, mean not only culturewide fame, but fame because of the relevance of these actions to struggles of Black America (Wallace became a national political figure, after all, because of his resistance to integration). The obsessive need to win, to dominate another, is the epitome of macho, and both Aaron and Bremer fit the pattern perfectly.

This general connection is confirmed by particular intersections of memorabilia and rolling text. One of these is evident in one of the stills from

Benning as a Milwaukee Brave, the poster image for *American Dreams*.

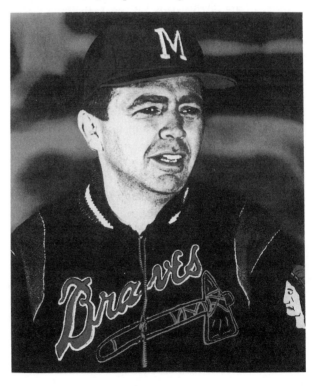

American Dreams that Benning had printed: Bremer's comment, "the 1st person I held a conversation with in 3 months was a near naked girl rubbing my erect penis...," is in the process of rolling across the screen as we see a card on which Hank Aaron's body parts (though not a penis!) are printed: kids were to press out the body parts and assemble the baseball star. There are other, similar intersections between the Aaron memorabilia and the rolling text, and their implications are extended by a second set of intersections between the Aaron and Bremer motifs and the songs and speeches on the soundtrack. Benning describes one of these: "When Bremer talks about how the danger of driving over 80 mph with a bad front tire gave him an erection, the speech on the soundtrack is LBJ talking about escalating the Vietnam War."[2]

Benning relates this pattern to the recent history of critical film by revealing his own complicity with it, in several ways. The fact that he rewrote the excerpts from Bremer's diary in his own handwriting was a way of implying a certain kinship with Bremer or at least an interest in metaphorically reexperiencing Bremer's actions (there's even a certain obsessiveness in turning the printed text of Bremer's published diary back into handwriting; Bremer handwrote the diary, Benning does too, spelling errors and all). The fact of Benning's assembling a relatively complete collection of the Aaron memorabilia and presenting it to us, item by item, front and back (back, even when an item has information only on the front), while dramatically drawing attention to details so minor that only a collector would notice them, suggests a somewhat obsessive interest in Aaron's career. This is confirmed by the fact that for the premiere of *American Dreams* at Film Forum in New York, Benning designed a poster of himself in a Braves warm-up jacket he had made. And, most important, the fact that Benning devised a structure for the film that proceeds relentlessly from the opening moment, challenging the viewer not only to take in more than usual amounts of information, but to stay with a single, ongoing set of cinematic gestures, was a way of suggesting that his own career as a filmmaker – and the careers of other filmmakers in the largely male field of "structural film" – parallels the careers of Aaron and Bremer.[3] What the bat was to Aaron, and the gun was to Bremer, the camera and movie theater are to Benning.

Unlike *Riddles of the Sphinx*, *American Dreams* does not suggest much in the way of positive gender-political action. Although we may understand where Benning's sympathies lie, he remains an observer of history. However, *American Dreams* and Benning's other films do reveal his awareness of the gender-political implications of both the conventional cinema and of a particular form of critical film practice with which he had identified himself.

The conventional cinema rarely reveals the psychic growth of the individuals who collaborate on commercial movies. Whatever individual changes the producers, directors, cinematographers, actors, and other contributors have undergone are subsumed within the economic necessities of the individual film product. Because critical films are often produced by individuals, particular projects chart the overall trajectories of these individuals' thinking. In *American Dreams* Benning goes a step further: We can see him rethinking his career and the attitudes and approaches that have generated his previous projects.

NOTES

1. An approach to narrative quite close to *8½ × 11* can be found in John Dos Passos's novels, especially *Manhattan Transfer* (1925) and *U.S.A.* (1938).
2. See the James Benning interview in Scott MacDonald, *A Critical Cinema 2* (Berkeley, CA: University of California Press, 1992), p. 243.
3. P. Adams Sitney defined "Structural Film," in *Visionary Film* (New York: Oxford University Press, 1974), Chapter 12.

9
Su Friedrich
The Ties That Bind

During the 1970s and 1980s, it became increasingly common for filmmakers and those viewers familiar with avant-garde film to reject both the personal cinema epitomized by Stan Brakhage and Jonas Mekas and the structural film of Snow, Gehr, and Paul Sharits, on the grounds that these approaches were as ideologically reactionary as the conventional cinema they pretended to critique. Despite their unconventional style, many of the personal films were as fully centered on the mythic struggles of white men as any industry genre film; and structural filmmakers fetishized equipment and processes to which women had limited access: They were a bunch of men "playing with their tools."[1] Some filmmakers – Mulvey/Wollen and Benning, among them – attempted to recondition elements of the rejected practices, in the hope of producing film experiences that would simultaneously critique the commercial cinema and reactionary dimensions of other film-critical practices. And there were other responses as well.

There was the "punk" or "new-wave" response by Beth B and Scott B, Vivienne Dick, and others, who abjured personal, "poetic" intimacy and fascination with the filmic apparatus in favor of visceral, often raunchy film experiences dealing with current issues, produced on the most inexpensive available technology, and aimed at new, adventurous film audiences that assembled in unconventional places (rock bars, for example) and at unconventional times (at midnight showings). There was also interest in a feminist cinema that avoided not only anything that might be interpreted as exploitation of the female body, but all forms of sensual film pleasure that had been nurtured during the patriarchal history of commercial and alternative cinema. Examples include Mulvey/Wollen's *Penthesilea* (Mulvey sometimes calls it a "scorched earth film"); Yvonne Rainer's *Journeys from*

Berlin/1971 (focus of Chapter 14 of this volume); and Su Friedrich's *Cool Hands, Warm Heart* (1979), which documents several women performing conventional, but normally private women's rituals – one woman shaves her legs, another shaves her armpits, a third braids her hair – on a crowded street on the Lower East Side, as a way of rebelling against canons of "femininity" and "good taste" in commercial media and against those avant-garde filmmakers who argue that films shouldn't polemicize an identifiable politic. In such films, traditional viewer enjoyment is replaced by the pleasure of defying the tradition of cinema as an apolitical sensual arena.[2]

By the 1980s, Friedrich was becoming convinced that the rejection of personal filmmaking, structural filmmaking, or other approaches did not "liberate" cinema in any practical sense; it simply narrowed the options. The issue was not to avoid the personal or the systematic, but to reappropriate and reenergize as many useful dimensions of the previous film-critical practices as possible. Indeed, the consolidation of traditionally distinct arenas of independent film was to become one of Friedrich's characteristic strategies. *The Ties That Bind* was the first film in which this strategy was obvious.

The focus of *The Ties That Bind* is Friedrich's relationship with her mother, Lore Bucher Friedrich, who came of age in Ulm, Germany, in the 1930s amidst the rise of the Nazis, and, after the war, married an American GI and moved to Chicago, where they divorced in 1965. Unlike the other filmmakers discussed in this section, however, Friedrich doesn't simply review psychic developments that she has considered or experienced. Rather, the *making* of *The Ties That Bind* was a process of psychic exploration for which the finished film serves as an index. Friedrich's interest in making a film about her mother seems to have developed out of the self-questioning so common for German Americans following the Second World War and, especially, the revelation of the scope of the Holocaust. American commercial media had conventionally repressed such self-questioning – indeed, had relentlessly avoided the idea that Americans were in any sense complicit with the Nazis, who were conventionally depicted as nearly an alien species. For Friedrich, it was time to come to grips with her past, to see if there were ties that bound her, in any sense, to the Third Reich. She had never talked to her mother in any detail about her experiences in Ulm, partly for fear of what she might learn about her mother and, therefore, herself: If her mother had played a role in the Nazis' rise to power, Friedrich seems to have felt, she herself was in some sense complicit with the results of Nazi power, even if only genetically. For *The Ties That Bind* she was determined

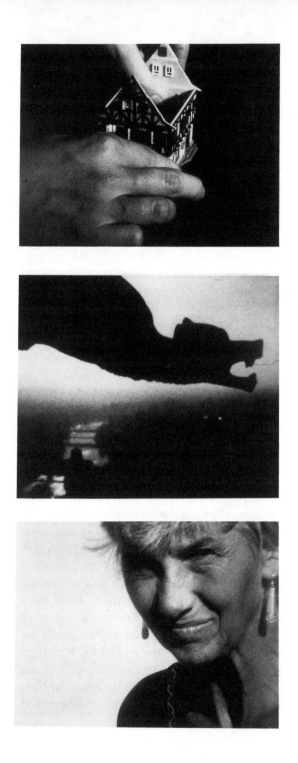

to find out as much of the truth as she could. The result was a sustained conversation with Lore Friedrich, excerpts of which provide the central organizing thread of the film.

The autobiographical dimension of *The Ties That Bind* is not only overt, it is presented in a manner that recalls various dimensions of the history of independent cinema in addition to the personal avant-garde tradition of the 1960s, mentioned earlier. The daughter's candid questioning of her mother about their shared past relates to that tradition within *cinéma vérité* documentary of filmmakers exploring their domestic environments: Instances include Martha Coolidge's *David: Off and On* (1973), Amalie Rothschild's *Nana, Mom, and Me* (1974), Ed Pincus's *Diaries* (1976), Michelle Citron's *Daughter Rite* (1978), Maxi Cohen's *Joe and Maxi* (1979), and Ross McElwee's *Backyard* (1982). There is nothing unusual in Friedrich's inclusion of the interview, in fact, except for her decision to embed it within a cinematic context characterized by a very wide range of film practices – a far larger range than is evident in the *cinéma vérité* films I've listed. Friedrich's questions are presented as hand-scratched texts – a reappropriation of the avant-garde tradition of hand-working the emulsion by Len Lye, the Kuchar Brothers, Stan Brakhage (in his titles and film signatures, as well as in his films), Carolee Schneemann, Walter Ungerer, Paul Sharits, Diana Barrie, and others *and* of the tradition of using printed or written text as a central visual element of a film: Lye's *Musical Poster No. 1* (1940), Paul Sharits's *Word Movie/Fluxfilm* (1966), *Zorns Lemma*, Snow's *So Is This* (1983), *American Dreams*, Friedrich's own *Gently Down the Stream* (1982) ... Since viewers must construct the questions, one word at a time, they become, in a sense, *our* questions as well as Friedrich's.

Lore Friedrich's memories are the central narrative of *The Ties That Bind,* but they are present only on the soundtrack (we do see imagery of Lore Friedrich in the visuals, but this imagery is a silent portrait that was filmed as a separate process from the interview). As she relates her memories (beginning at the moment when, as a child, she was becoming conscious of Hitler's rise to power, and proceeding chronologically to describe the results of her family's refusal to dissociate itself from its Jewish friends, the coming of the war, the arrival of the Allies, her meeting Paul Friedrich, and her early years in the United States), the film's visuals document a series of journeys by Su Friedrich, several of them having directly to do with her mother's history.

Hands construct a model of a German house; a gargoyle in Ulm; and Lore Friedrich, from Su Friedrich's *The Ties That Bind* (1984).

The most extensive of these journeys is Friedrich's trip to Ulm in 1982 to see what remains of the locations her mother recalls. Friedrich documented her trip with a Super-8mm camera, in black and white, in a handheld expressionist style reminiscent of Brakhage and Mekas. She visits her mother's house and other landmarks in Ulm; and she travels by train to Berlin (there are shots of the Wall) and to Dachau to see the concentration camp there. Once the material was transferred to 16mm, Friedrich used scratched texts to identify and clarify the imagery. On one level, the Super-8 material recalls the sorts of home-movie travel diaries so many of us make of our trips to unfamiliar places, but the inky look of this imagery and its relationship to her mother's frequently heartrending memories give it a very un-home-movie impact. A second journey documented in *The Ties That Bind*, this one in 16mm, is Su Friedrich's visit to the Seneca Army Depot in upstate New York to take part in, and record, a demonstration against militarism by the women encamped at the depot and a counterdemonstration by a crowd of flag-waving locals.

Lore Friedrich's history and Su Friedrich's journeys are contextualized by three other kinds of imagery. Periodically, we see someone – Friedrich, I assume – open a package containing a plastic model of a traditional Bavarian house, assemble the house, and finally set fire to it and stomp it to ruins in a pair of black leather boots: this imagery is arranged in a manner reminiscent of some of the replacement images in *Zorns Lemma*. A second type of imagery is filmed material from the past: a single-shot Edison film of a young woman dancing and waving an American flag; archival footage of Ulm in ruins after the Allied bombings; and home-movie footage of Lore and Paul Friedrich soon after their arrival in the United States. Still other shots record Friedrich at home, sitting on the toilet reading a newspaper, going through several pieces of neo-Nazi junk mail, and watching television shows and advertisements.

Su Friedrich's scratched questions and Lore Friedrich's spoken responses provide an overall rhythm within which the other kinds of information are interspersed at more or less regular intervals. Within any particular minute, we see many types of visual information; but over the duration of *The Ties That Bind* each type of information develops into a recognizable motif. Altogether, the several motifs articulate a roughly serial structure that is simultaneously reminiscent of films discussed in earlier chapters of this section *and* critical of their systematic rigidity. Though it is carefully constructed, *The Ties That Bind* is far more fluid than *Zorns Lemma*, *Riddles of the Sphinx*, and *American Dreams*. Friedrich's use of an overall serial structure throws the hand-held expressionism of her camerawork into clear relief, and vice versa.

Friedrich's commitment to a synthesis of approaches in *The Ties That Bind* – to a formal synergy – is not only reflected in her inclusion of elements of several cinematic traditions usually seen as distinct, at least in North America; it is also evident in the way these diverse elements are arranged within the film. On one level, the viewer is involved in constructing a set of continuities from the serial presentation of diverse strands of information. At the same time, however, Friedrich makes clear from the opening moments of the film that her visual imagery and her auditory imagery are perceptually and conceptually intersecting all the time, to form an increasingly complex and suggestive cinematic weave. Friedrich's consistent refusal to use sync sound is an emblem of her critique of commercial cinema's methods and of the ideologies these methods have conventionally supported, but it simultaneously provides her with a means of developing new forms of pleasure that can invigorate multiple viewings of the film.

Any passage of the *The Ties That Bind* could be used to exemplify Friedrich's intricate sound–image structuring. As the film begins, Lore Friedrich is telling of her first awareness of the Nazis and Hitler, during a subjective camera shot from inside a tunnel out into the light. The intersection of Lore Friedrich's spoken memory and Su Friedrich's visual memory creates a variety of implications. Most obviously, perhaps, the visual imagery is a metaphor for young Lore Friedrich's developing awareness: She moves from darkness to light, as Frampton and the audience do in *Zorns Lemma*. If one thinks of the intersection as a reference to Su Friedrich, however, it seems to suggest *her* coming out of the darkness into the light about her mother's past. The birth implications of Friedrich's movement out of a tunnel are relevant in both a general sense (Su Friedrich is listening to the woman who gave birth to her) and in a more immediate sense. Su Friedrich's decision to make the film we are watching has been a rebirth: As the mother delivers the facts of her childhood to her daughter, the daughter's sense of her own past, and her current identity, is reconstructed. In addition to the many metaphoric implications of this intersection of sound and image, the particulars of the movement of camera and imagery often correspond to specific nuances of Lore Friedrich's voice.

As *The Ties That Bind* proceeds, hundreds of significant intersections are revealed. In fact, developing this network of connections among the film's visual and auditory motifs was the central focus of the 700 hours Friedrich claims to have spent editing the film.[3] In some cases, particular types of intersections are articulated during extended passages, and sometimes through the entire film. One of the most suggestive sets of intersections is the juxtaposition of Lore Friedrich's memories and Su Friedrich's record of her visit to the Seneca Army Depot. In one instance, Lore Friedrich is talking about the cruelty of the Allies during their "liberation" of Ulm, especially their cruelty to older people; she exclaims, "That people can live and be so brutal!" Just after Lore Friedrich's emotional memory, we see a sign at the Seneca Depot demonstration that reads: "Nuke them till they glow, then shoot them in the dark." The callousness of the sign demonstrates that our current world is full of people capable of the kind of cruelty that shocked Lore Friedrich; and this is one of a series of intersections that suggest similarities between the Germany of the 1930s and the United States of the late 1970s and early 1980s, including widespread jingoistic patriotism and assumptions on the part of large segments of the population about the "correct" status of women – assumptions demonstrated by Lore Friedrich's experiences in the two countries. When her father died in Germany, her dreams of attending college to study music died with him (her guardian claimed there was only money enough for secretarial school); when she married Paul Friedrich and came to the United States, her dreams were revived, only to be put on hold while Paul Friedrich found his way into the postwar economy, then destroyed still again, when he asked for a divorce: We see Lore Friedrich working as a secretary in Su Friedrich's portrait of her. The text that concludes the film tells us, "In 1980 (after raising three children alone) she bought herself a piano and began to practice the scales."

For Friedrich the completion of *The Ties That Bind* was evidence of her achievement of a level of psychic maturity that wouldn't have been possible without the film. Her physical journeys to visit her mother in Chicago, to Germany to explore their shared past, and to the Seneca Army Depot to explore their shared political present were necessary stages in Friedrich's psychic journey through the barriers of fear and ignorance that had separated her from her mother. And in the finished film, this movement through barriers is evident on all levels. *The Ties That Bind* carries viewers across the barriers between mother and daughter, between the past and present, between continents, between "distinct" forms of alternative film practice, and between separate visuals and soundtrack toward a film experience that grows increasingly coherent and whole in direct proportion to the attention it is accorded. The complex network of interconnections between the many facets of the film become "the ties that bind" the film, and the viewer's experience of it, together.

Friedrich's interest in combining disparate forms of film as a means of modeling the struggle toward psychocinematic wholeness has remained the hallmark of her approach. In fact, with *Sink or Swim* this tendency reached a metalevel: The newer film recontextualizes and elaborates on *The Ties That Bind*. In *Sink or Swim* Friedrich returned to her family history as a way of coming to terms with her relationship with her father, of whom she saw little after he divorced her mother. Again, she uses diverse kinds of imagery – hand-held, often gestural imagery of children, recycled home movies, footage from educational films – and develops an intricate network of intersections between this visual imagery and a set of stories from her childhood narrated by a young girl. In this film, however, the overall structure is more precisely and obviously systematic. If the fluid structure of *The Ties That Bind* suggests Lore Friedrich's ability and necessity to learn to adjust to continually evolving circumstances, to "go with the flow," the structure of *Sink or Swim* is reflective of Friedrich's experiences of the rigidity of her father, the well-known linguist/anthropologist Paul Friedrich. *Sink or Swim* is divided into twenty-six sections (there's also a final coda) arranged in reverse alphabetical order according to the titles of the sections – "zygote," "Y chromosome," "X chromosome," "witness," "virgin" . . . – as an overt reference to her father's profession. That the letters are in reverse

Imagery for *A* ("Athena/Atalanta/Aphrodite"), from Friedrich's *Sink or Swim* (1990).

order suggests that her psychic development required Friedrich to unlearn as much as she learned from him.

This more rigorously systematic structure may also be an implicit reference to one of Friedrich's cinematic "fathers": Hollis Frampton and the alphabetically arranged *Zorns Lemma*. As in *The Ties That Bind,* however, the primary focus of Friedrich's critique is the conventional cinema. Indeed, the opening, "zygote" sequence, though only one minute forty-three seconds long, can be read as a witty encapsulation of conventional film history. "Zygote" uses a series of shots recycled from old instructional films: Friedrich intercuts between images of eggs and images of sperm, then shows an egg being fertilized and beginning to develop. As the physical reality of fertilization – the potential beginning of a family – is presented in microscopic enlargement, the narrator describes the circumstances of one of Western culture's first mythical families, that of Zeus and Hera. Precisely when the child narrator describes how Zeus was married to Hera, the original cell inside a fertilized egg divides into two, and the narrator's brief review of Zeus's other extramarital relationships and offspring is emphasized dramatically by the cells continuing to divide in the egg. This passage is a witty comment on commercial cinema from D. W. Griffith on: What is more central to conventional movie pleasure than a dramatic chase, expressed through intercutting, that leads to a maintenance and confirmation not only of the species, but of conventional definitions of gender and family? The fact that, once the egg in "zygote" is fertilized, we see the cells bifurcate again and again, in conjunction with the story of Zeus's love affairs and illegitimate children, extends Friedrich's comment on conventional cinema: In the decades since Griffith, adultery has become a central dimension in North American film. Indeed, as often as not, the eroticized female body is the payoff for the male-gendered movie viewer, and the very fact of looking at conventional films becomes a form of repressed adultery: Just as so many men *in* films have sex with more than one woman (a situation cinema-historically less frequent and more dangerous for women), the male or "male" spectators come to "know" the women in films in addition to whatever women they know in real life.

Essentially, *The Ties That Bind* and *Sink or Swim* are Friedrich's attempts to rethink gender, especially insofar as it relates to parenthood. Each film suggests the limitations of the traditional gender definitions marketed by conventional cinema. Friedrich's mother's life has been constricted again and again by circumstances over which she has had no control. And yet, Lore Friedrich not only survives with dignity but successfully sees her children to better lives. She is never able to return to college to study music, but her children are able to attend college, and, indeed, her creative urges are embodied in Su Friedrich's filmmaking career: *The Ties That Bind* and *Sink or Swim* are, essentially, emblems of Lore Friedrich's final victory. On the other hand, Paul Friedrich's life, while also determined in important ways by circumstances beyond his control (he met Lore Friedrich while stationed in Germany immediately after World War II), is characterized by opportunity and achievement. He attends college and becomes a widely known scholar; and yet, his success reveals (to his daughter) a pattern of callousness and self-indulgence that reconfirms the most conventional cultural stereotypes of "maleness."

For Su Friedrich, the only solution is to pursue a life and a filmmaking career that reiterates neither parent's successes or failures, but combines elements of both their lives into a new and productive psychic amalgam. This solution is implicit in the imagery that accompanies the only two sections of *Sink or Swim* that are not accompanied by sound: "Y chromosome" and "X chromosome." The imagery for "Y chromosome" is an exquisite textural shot of a white fluffy material, a close-up of a milkweed pod being opened by a hand. The imagery in "X chromosome" is a shot of an elephant's trunk picking up a peanut. On one level this imagery is fitting for the gender of the Y (male) and X (female) chromosomes: The hand in "Y chromosome" is scattering seeds, and the elephant is ingesting a seed. And yet, at the same time, the imagery defies standard gender expectations: The soft, textural quality of the imagery in "Y chromosome" and the phallic quality of the elephant's trunk might lead any viewer not clear about the gender of X and Y chromosomes to identify the shots incorrectly. As these shots suggest, the crucial issue for Friedrich is using film to help reconstruct our understanding of what gender means so that we can see that each woman and man combines both genders and that in this combination they are more fundamentally alike than different. Only by coming to terms with what unites us can we contribute to a societal evolution that will provide both the continuity and the breadth of options all healthy human beings require.

NOTES

1. See Sitney's *Visionary Film*, Chapter 12.
2. There was also a commitment on the part of some filmmakers with roots in the avant-garde to make films that could be politically and/or formally radical *and* popular: Chantal Akerman's *Jeanne Dielman . . .* (1975), Lizzie Borden's *Working Girls* (1986), and Jim Jarmusch's *Stranger Than Paradise* are examples.
3. See Scott MacDonald, *A Critical Cinema 2* (Berkeley, CA: University of California Press, 1992), p. 295.

10
Yervant Gianikian and Angela Ricci Lucchi
From the Pole to the Equator

The films discussed in Part 2 reflect on and catalyze various psychic journeys. The characters *in* the films, whether they be cinematic incarnations of the filmmakers or figures clearly distinct from them, travel through the world, in some cases toward their own awareness and enlightenment, but always in directions that enlighten *us*. The personae of the filmmakers that can be deduced from the films' content, style, and structure have clearly made their own physical and psychic journeys; the films are direct or deflected indices of them. And for the audience, the films create experiences that have the potential for transforming how films – conventional films and critical films – are seen and understood. It can be argued that, in general, conventional film entertainment is propaganda for the status quo. For the filmmakers discussed in this volume, the challenge of filmmaking is confronting the ideology of the status quo and its articulation in cinema, and, to the extent possible, instigating a progressive reformation of the film experience. None of the filmmakers discussed so far fits this pattern more clearly than the Italians, Yervant Gianikian and Angela Ricci Lucchi. Their film, *From the Pole to the Equator,* uses filmed material (which originally functioned, for all practical purposes, as propaganda affirming the ideological status quo of early twentieth-century Italy) as the raw material with which to fashion not only a revaluation of the particular information originally recorded in this "raw material," but a more progressive sense of the world in general.

Although *From the Pole to the Equator* recycles early film material, it is not – like their earlier *Karagoez-Catalogo 9.5* (1981) – a compilation of miscellaneous, interesting footage. Rather, it is a systematic reworking of film material made by early Italian cinematographer/filmmaker Luca Comerio (1874–1940), who was active as a cinematographer by 1905 and continued to make and collect films after World War I. Comerio was involved in dozens of films, of a variety of kinds. In 1908 the success of his fiction film *Rocambole* allowed him to establish one of the most successful Italian production companies. The title of the Gianikian/Ricci Lucchi film derives from another Comerio film, *From the Pole to the Equator,* an elaborate montage made from earlier films Comerio had shot and/or collected, edited at some point during the 1920s. For Gianikian and Ricci Lucchi, the most fascinating dimension of Comerio was his willingness to travel to remote areas of the world in the service of audiences hungry for exotic people and places. He is emblematic of the first wave of cine-explorers for whom the motion picture camera was simultaneously a means for escaping the familiar and reconfirming it.

Between 1981 and 1985, Gianikian and Ricci Lucchi acquired the Comerio archives and proceeded to try to save the nitrate originals while at the same time recycling them into their own work.[1] For *From the Pole to the Equator,* they reprinted 35mm Comerio materials, frame by frame, onto 16mm stock, tinted (and in some instances hand-painted) the imagery, edited the sequences, and finally commissioned a soundtrack by Californians Keith Ullrich and Charles Anderson. The resulting film "saves" the original Comerio materials, which were in a dangerous state of decay when Gianikian and Ricci Lucchi obtained them, and provides a sense of the considerable power of Comerio's accomplishments. Of course, with the passing of nearly a century, the Comerio materials had sustained various kinds of damage that remain evident in the Gianikian/Ricci Lucchi film. Rather than detracting from the film, however, this damage provides a historical "frame" that adds to the poignancy of the film's impact, in a manner reminiscent of Gehr's *Eureka.*.

From the Pole to the Equator divides into passages not explicitly distinguished in the visuals, though they are usually signaled by changes in the music. Generally speaking, each passage is determined by a specific geographic locale. The opening section (most of the sections are from seven to ten minutes long; the final section is around fifteen minutes; the complete film is ninety-six minutes) was filmed first from a train snaking through the Alps and subsequently from an Alpine tram car descending into a village. The following section presents imagery Comerio filmed during an exploratory voyage to the South Pole. The focus is on the explorers observing and killing polar animals. The third section was shot at the frontier of the Russian and Persian empires; in general, its focus is on a local army that was ap-

113

parently working with the visiting Italians. The next section reveals Italian soldiers and church people working among African peoples: Africans dance for the Europeans, march in Europeanized outfits; a child is baptized; a group of African children follow a nun's orders in a school. The film moves to India where we see street scenes, life along country roads, a woman dancing for the camera, a parade of European royalty and military, and the activities of Buddhist monks; then returns to African locations: first Tangiers, where we see street and harbor scenes, and later, after a series of portraits, to Eritrea where local people seem to be performing a series of mock battles for the camera; and finally to Uganda, where Baron Franchetti – according to Gianikian and Ricci Lucchi, "the Italian version of T. E. Lawrence" – kills a variety of animals (generally we see Franchetti shooting and the animals in the throes of death) and moves his entourage from place to place with the help of dozens of Africans. The final section of the film presents footage from World War I: Soldiers marching, riding horses and bicycles, and fighting in the field; in a number of instances we see soldiers die. Just at the end of the section we see a panoramic view of the words "VIVA IL RE" ("Long Live the King") spelled out by sheep herded together. The film ends with a shot of a nobleman holding a rabbit just out of the reach of dogs, to his own amusement and that of several women.

In a sense, the imagery Gianikian and Ricci Lucchi reprinted for *From the Pole to the Equator* is exciting to look at, not only because of its obvious historical importance and because of their dexterity in refashioning it for their own purposes, but because Comerio was a remarkable cinematographer. In fact, for many modern viewers, Gianikian/Ricci Lucchi have uncovered a paradox: The horror of what we see in the footage – the relentless destruction of animals, the death of men during wartime, the domination of foreign cultures by military means – is presented to us in footage that was, and remains, very beautiful. There is nothing "primitive" in this primitive cinema except the ways in which the men who are its subjects relate to the world. Since Gianikian and Ricci Lucchi have reworked and reorganized Comerio's original footage, we cannot be sure from seeing *From the Pole to the Equator* how Comerio edited the imagery he collected on his journeys, but his remarkable sense of composition is obvious in nearly every shot – from the dramatic pans over Alpine landscape during the train rides that open the film, to the exquisite portraits of people from non-European cultures, to the dramatic use of mattes during the hunting se-

Italians in Africa, from Yervant Gianikian and Angela Ricci Lucchi's *From the Pole to the Equator* (1987).

quences in Antarctica and Uganda. At one point in his career, Comerio apparently had aspirations to be Mussolini's official filmmaker, the way Leni Riefenstahl later became the official filmmaker for the Third Reich; and certainly the power of his cinematography, as well as the ideology implicit within it, qualified him for such a role.

For Gianikian and Ricci Lucchi, the Comerio materials and the historical period they capture and epitomize presented a serious challenge. As was true for Su Friedrich in *The Ties That Bind,* the relationship of Gianikian and Ricci Lucchi to the dimension of their ethnic heritage represented in the Comerio footage was problematic. But while Friedrich could lay many of her suspicions and fears to rest by talking with her mother, the Comerio materials were a *fait accompli:* what had happened had happened and no amount of contemporary embarrassment could change it. The question was how to accept the reality of the past without accepting its ideology, how to cinematically present what Comerio had accomplished as an explorer/ cinematographer without betraying the humane ideals of the present.

Over the years, critical filmmakers have developed a variety of tactics for recycling the problematic past into a more ideologically palatable present. The most obvious, perhaps, is that developed by Bruce Conner, who discovered that by decontextualizing imagery from a previous film and surrounding it with excerpts from other films that have no necessary relationship to the imagery, other than what is implicit in his esthetic, he could entirely transform the impact and meaning both of the original imagery and the imagery that surrounded it. A different tactic is explored in Ken Jacobs's *Tom, Tom, the Piper's Son,* David Rimmer's *Seashore* (1971), and Martin Arnold's *Pièce Touchee* (1989): Here the filmmakers visually "analyze" particular earlier films by devising rigorous formal procedures that allow viewers to re-see the original material slowed down, in new framings, over and over. Still another related tactic is evident in the Kuchar brothers' early films, mentioned in the introduction, where gestures from conventional films are reenacted but in a low-budget, homemade manner that implicitly reveals the socioeconomic ideology of the conventional gestures in the obvious gaps between original and remake.

The tactic chosen by Gianikian and Ricci Lucchi is most closely related to the Jacobs/Rimmer/Arnold approach. They decided they would accept the actual imagery, frame for frame, *but* they would re-form (and reform) it by controlling the speed with which the viewer sees the frames. In essence, they did a motion study of the Comerio materials. Or, to put this another way, instead of simply allowing us to *see* the Comerio materials, Gianikian and Ricci Lucchi enable us to both *see* them and *see through* them. The result is that we witness the quest of early twentieth-century Italians to penetrate the Third World and to challenge the wilderness, *and* (implicitly) the journey of consciousness that ultimately led to Gianikian and Ricci Lucchi's horror at the events of this period.

Throughout *From the Pole to the Equator* the imagery seems to hover between a series of stills and conventional film motion. It is as though we continually relive Muybridge's discovery that he could analyze movement into still photographs and then resynthesize the stills into the illusion of normal motion. In fact, this dimension of the film is reminiscent of Thom Andersen's use of a similar procedure in *Eadweard Muybridge, Zooprax-ographer:* Andersen repeatedly shows a sequence of Muybridge stills and then accelerates them into motion. The decision by Gianikian/Ricci Lucchi to withhold conventional motion has a variety of effects. For one thing, it is a function and reminder of the fact that the celluloid strip of film images is always a grid. Although the overall organization of *From the Pole to the Equator* does not arrange passages of imagery into an obvious grid structure the way *Zorns Lemma, Riddles of the Sphinx,* and *American Dreams* do, and does not even suggest a grid the way Friedrich's arrangement of visual motifs in *The Ties That Bind* does, the film's consistently erratic motion is an index of the fact that when Gianikian and Ricci Lucchi reprinted Comerio's imagery, they dealt with it one frame at a time, the way Muybridge built his grids of still photographs, one image at a time.

The slowed pace of the imagery also emphasizes the fact that, in many instances, Comerio's imagery was recorded in relatively long takes. Because of the slowed speed of the imagery, in fact, *From the Pole to the Equator* is more Lumièresque than Comerio's original material. It is clear from the opening moments that for Gianikian and Ricci Lucchi their film is a journey back to the beginnings of cinema. Indeed, the long train rides that open the film are a reference to the Lumières' *L'Arrivée du train en gare* and to the interest of early film audiences in cinema travel: both in the experience of moving from one place to another and in the worlds such "travel" made accessible. As we begin *From the Pole to the Equator,* the camera, the viewer, and Cinema are on the move, recording the adventures of the industrialized nations within which motion picture technologies had developed.

The decision to modulate the rate at which viewers see Comerio's imagery and to consistently withhold normal motion has particular as well as general effects. In fact, it is the particular effects that allow *From the Pole to the Equator* to function as a sustained critique of the ideology embedded within Comerio's original imagery, and, by implication, within much of the imagery consumed by contemporary viewers during conventional movie experiences. With the exception of the World War I footage of Italians fighting in the Alps, the two main foci of *From the Pole to the Equator* are the peoples of Africa and the East and the animals of Africa and Antarctica. Presumably, the original imagery of hunting we see in the early Antarctic sequences and later in Africa was meant to convey the excitement of the sport and the prowess of the hunters: The hunters' technology has made them more powerful, more "fit to survive," than even the most imposing animals. But, while viewers may recognize Comerio's attitudes about hunting, Gianikian and Ricci Lucchi's reworking of the Comerio imagery subverts his intent. By slowing the pace of a female polar bear's desperate battle to save her cub, so that viewers can understand *her* intent and empathize with *her* terror and courage, Gianikian and Ricci Lucchi undercut the hunters' claim to evolutionary superiority: The hunters seem simply insensitive and brutal. Protected by their boat and their guns, they mercilessly slaughter beautiful creatures: The hunters become the "animals"; the animals are recognized as "peoples" under attack.

Similarly, Gianikian/Ricci Lucchi's modulation of Comerio's imagery of "primitive" societies puts us more deeply in touch with the "exotics" than with the "civilized" Italians. Near the end of the third section, for example, a young woman and man perform a folk dance in front of a crowd of people presumably native to the region. In the middle of the crowd sit two men: One appears to be some sort of elder representative of these people; the other, an Italian military officer, is presumably the guest of honor. Everyone in the shot seems interested in the dancers, and for good reason: Their exotic movements, which are emphasized by the slowed pace of Gianikian and Ricci Lucchi's presentation, are fascinating. Everyone seems interested, that is, *except* the Italian officer, who stares offscreen, oblivious to the dance, daydreaming, one might infer, about future conquests or more "civilized" surroundings. In general, the Italians seem bored and boring, humorless and pretentious throughout the film. Whereas the individuals in the "exotic" cultures seem to enjoy what they do and seem pleased to perform for the camera, the Italians seem interested only in the spectacle of domination: they raise their guns to shoot, stand around rigidly in their military uniforms, ride in military parades.

The subtle "analysis" provided by Gianikian and Ricci Lucchi's precise modulation of the speed of the individual frames of Comerio's imagery (and by the more conventional gestures of their editing) is confirmed and extended by the soundtrack and by their use of color. The Anderson/Ullrich music is eerie, haunting; it tends to emphasize the grimness of the events depicted, even in instances where the imagery itself seems relatively neutral. The music helps to convey a sense of overwhelming sadness about what was lost through the colonization and domination of people and animals. It also periodically dramatizes our historical complicity in the events; at times, the native peoples seem to dance to the music *we're* hearing, particularly during the passages filmed in Africa. These momentary synchronizations of image and sound reaffirm a fact that is implicit throughout: We, sitting in a theater, fascinated with the people and events Comerio has captured, are the benefactors not only of his filmmaking, but of the processes of power and domination he documents for us. In fact, Comerio's footage dramatizes – as fully as any early footage I've seen – the degree to which the camera is one of the spearheads of empire. The Africans and Indians dance to the beat of *our* drum as fully as they danced for the conquerors, and in a historical sense we're probably no more prepossessing than the soldiers and church people whose commitment to colonization many of us are likely to abhor.

The schizoid quality of *From the Pole to the Equator* is emphasized by the obvious pains Gianikian and Ricci Lucchi took with color. In a general sense their color is reminiscent of that used in early film: monochrome

Indian woman dancing in *From the Pole to the Equator.*

119

tinting, and in a few instances, hand-coloring, frame by frame. But the way in which the color is articulated is different from the use of color in the contemporary prints of early films I'm aware of. Most of *From the Pole to the Equator* is tinted but, while the color is monochromatic within any given frame, the color varies from moment to moment. A passage may be green, but the quality of green continually changes. More dramatic shifts in color separate sections of the film from each other (the move from the train section to the Antarctic section early in the film is signaled by a change from green-tinted imagery to blue-tinted imagery): However, dramatic shifts in color can occur anytime during a passage, and in some cases within a continuous shot. In other words, the use of tinting is not tied to the specifics of the content, as it is for example in D. W. Griffith's films.

The color in those infrequent passages when Gianikian and Ricci Lucchi forgo tinting for multitoned hand-coloring is realistic, but the fact of its being embedded in passages of tinted imagery renders it different in impact from a Méliès hand-colored film. The fact that the more painstaking use of multiple colors is confined to the section documenting India is probably no accident: The majority of multicolored moments seem to relate to the activities of Buddhist monks. It may be that Gianikian and Ricci Lucchi highlight the monks because, of all the Comerio imagery they reprinted, these images most nearly represent the philosophic opposite of the imperial quest so powerfully documented during the remainder of the film. Overall, like the color in Peter Kubelka's *Unsere Afrikareise* (*Our African Journey* – with which the Gianikian/Ricci Lucchi film shares much), the color in *From the Pole to the Equator* has a double impact that befits the film's complex mood: it makes the film more sensuously beautiful, more watchable, so that we can more deeply experience the horror it captures.

Instead of reconfirming the contemporary status quo, as most conventional filmmakers do, even when they're dealing with the past, Gianikian and Ricci Lucchi provide viewers with a cinematic excursion into the early history of film that recontextualizes Luca Comerio's visual record of his far-flung journeying so that we can hardly help but recognize that our contemporary film experiences are extensions of cultural and political developments from which we might well wish to dissociate ourselves. My guess is that Gianikian and Ricci Lucchi would hope that our experience with their exploration and cinematic subversion of Luca Comerio's imagery, and the ideology it embodies, might lead viewers to question the representation of other cultures in all forms of film, and particularly in those mass-market movies that tend to garner national attention, where the adventurer from the "civilized world" wreaks havoc on nonindustrialized peoples, overturning their homes and marketplaces, for the viewers' excitement and amusement. As chilling as Comerio's images can be, they are at least open about their ideology and political goals. Too often, contemporary audiences for commercial film are entertained by the spectacle of imperial domination and destruction without needing to recognize that any political agenda is involved, or that the exploits of Indiana Jones et al. are merely symbolic representations of realities as grim as those revealed in *From the Pole to the Equator*.

NOTE

1. My information about Gianikian and Ricci Lucchi's methods comes from in-person discussions with them.

Part III

Premonitions of a Global Cinema

One of the first urges of the Lumières was to send camerapeople to faraway places, and some early narrative filmmakers (Chaplin, for example) saw cinema as having as much potential as music to be the quintessential *international* art form. Nevertheless, during most of film history, entertainment films have tended to be culture-bound, confined by the limits of geography and language. There seems to have been no point during the early decades of cinema history – and not much has changed in this regard – when the production and exhibition of films was in any real sense a meaningful interchange between cultures. Of course, the onset of the sound film confirmed this tendency. If it had been difficult for foreign films to find their way to American audiences before 1927 – because of the control American film producers maintained over exhibitors and because Hays Office standards tended, in effect, to protect the local industry at the expense of foreign cinema – the added cost of making English versions of films rendered any foreign response to the dominant American industry nearly impossible. Film remained "international" only in the sense that American film producers had the resources to exploit foreign markets (as an adjunct to the primary American market), and other, European industries could exploit audiences outside their national borders (as an adjunct to their primary markets). It was a rare event when a product from a smaller national market found an audience in a country dominated by its own national industry. "Internationalism" took the form of economic imperialism, not cultural exchange.

As film history solidified into a pattern of separate national cinemas, a few of which had the resources to attract audiences in other nations, some viewers who had had the opportunity to see the products of more than one national film industry (and who had come to feel that quality filmmaking was not inevitably proportional to the economic power of a given national industry) reacted by forming film societies (or ciné-clubs), one main function of which was to offer audiences an ongoing international film experience. And, given the implicit critique of the status quo inherent in the efforts of film-society directors, it is not surprising that their more catholic interest in cinema included films of a variety of forms, as well as of a variety of national origins. Although the film-society movement is no longer as vital as it was from the 1920s through the 1950s (its success in different nations peaked during different decades), vestiges remain in North America and abroad, providing a relatively small audience with an ongoing critique of the nationalism of commercial film exhibition.

Another internationalizing force during recent decades especially has been the success of an increasing number of international film festivals, where producers, distributors, and exhibitors gather to energize the international market, primarily for commercial films. Currently, these festivals result in commercial films from a variety of nations – including areas of Africa, Latin America, and Asia traditionally marginalized by the American and European industries – being more widely available. Further, the access of individuals within most developed cultures to television sets, videocassette recorders and cable and satellite networks increasingly provides options for seeing some of the products of a variety of national film industries and, less often, of films made independently.

Regardless of these developments, however, film remains nationally bound, especially in the area of production. Whereas the plots of many films cross international boundaries, often necessitating the movement of the apparatus of production from one nation to another, the essential pattern is not very different from the distribution/exhibition patterns established during the first decades of film history. That is, particular production groups from the richer industries in the wealthier nations tend to move into foreign locations to take advantage of lower production costs and of "exotic" extras and atmosphere, and once the needs of the production are met, the groups withdraw. The peoples in the exotic locations have little input into the film, except for the labor and the atmosphere they provide. Even when there is an indigenous film industry, its production apparatus is rarely able to exploit the peoples of the richer nations in a fashion analogous to the way *they* are used. Not surprisingly, the realities of this inequality in production are reflected in the finished films. Foreign peoples, especially exotic peoples, and almost inevitably people from nonindustrialized areas of the world – and whatever struggles they are involved in – are rarely more than background for the adventures of the cinema heroes from industrially developed nations.

As is evident in earlier chapters of this book, the very success of mass-market movies does tend to catalyze critical responses. And though it is doubtful that these responses have much impact on the popular cinema, they do offer at least some portion of the audience the pleasure and insight of progressive alternatives, and opportunities for seeing many dimensions of the commercial cinema more clearly, including its characteristic nationalism. In recent years, many critical filmmakers have explored the possibility of film practices that defy international boundaries. Of course, the most obvious international approach is that epitomized by Soviet–Armenian filmmaker Artavazd Peleshyan, whose montage films – *Menkh* ("We," 1969), *Tarva Yeghaknere* ("The Seasons," 1975), *Mer Dar* ("Our Century," 1982, 1990) and others – often focus on Armenians in particular, as a means of exploring essential human issues common to many, if not all, cultures. Many critical filmmakers, and some industry directors, might consider themselves instances of this kind of internationalism.

The filmmakers discussed in the following chapters, however, approach the issue of internationalism more literally. They redirect the resources of a particular advantaged nation to promote cinematic worlds that demonstrate, or at least imply, the efficacy of moving through the very boundaries that have been so crucial in the production of these resources. And if their success in developing channels whereby other, "cinematically disadvantaged" cultures can express themselves to audiences beyond *their* boundaries has been at best very limited, some of the filmmakers have begun to explore filmmaking processes that – one can hope – will lead toward a cinema that functions more fully as a vehicle for escaping a narrow range of cultural attitudes. Brakhage has demonstrated that film can function to subvert the very conventions of human sight it was developed to confirm; the filmmakers discussed in this section suggest that film can subvert its own history as a weapon in the service of nationalism.

11
Warren Sonbert
The Carriage Trade

Like the other filmmakers discussed in Part 3, Warren Sonbert's international travels have been central in the production of his films. But unlike Luca Comerio, Sonbert does not seem to assume that his journeys to other sectors of the globe articulate a particular political ideology or imperial quest. Indeed, Sonbert has declared his opposition to political art in no uncertain terms: "Now it is quite possible to hide behind being a Gayist, a Feminist, or a Marxist and still be a lousy artist. Art is tied to Politics in absolutely no way whatsoever, or rather Art can be used by Politics, but Politics cannot be used by Art." At the same time, Sonbert recognizes that Art can be Politics, "in the sense of expanding horizons, broadening sensibilities, undermining the codes, being presented with multiple, often conflicting, points of view and the breakdown of rigidity."[1] In *The Carriage Trade,* and in much of the rest of his mature filmmaking, Sonbert simultaneously avoids direct cinematic comment on any political person or system while breaking radically with the conventional code that filmmaking is essentially a nationalistic enterprise. The result are film experiences that do not assume that one nation, one culture, or one language has, in any filmically significant sense, primacy over others.

The Carriage Trade was Sonbert's first long film (sixty-one minutes) and it remains his longest. In his catalogue description, he calls it his magnum opus.[2] *The Carriage Trade* reveals the basic approach to structure that was to distinguish all his subsequent films: It is a silent kaleidoscope of people and places, organized as an immense and subtle montage. In general, individual shots are brief – usually less than ten seconds, rarely more than fifteen. Conventional montages in commercial films function as intensifications and elaborations of the ongoing narrative developments within which they are embedded, and, as a result, one can often predict the nature

of successive images. *The Carriage Trade* reverses the usual relationship: The montage *is* the film; its fundamental continuity is a function of the filmmaker's perceptual and conceptual experiences, not of the activities of characters within a plot. Instead of embedding a montage within a narrative, Sonbert embeds shots that have at most minimal narrative elements within montage.

The Muybridge and Lumière approaches so central to the films in previous sections of this volume are evident in *The Carriage Trade* though they are less immediately obvious than in some of the films I've discussed. Overall, Sonbert's imagery is recorded with a Lumièresque straightforwardness and simplicity (though the shots are always recorded by a hand-held camera) and Sonbert's sudden shifts from one country to another, and from one continent to another, are similar to the shifts in geography from one exotic scene to another in early Lumière shows. Generally speaking, whether particular types of imagery were originally recorded in continuous shots or in sequences edited in-camera, they are organized into the overall montage so that we see any given subject "analyzed" into successive segments that are interspersed over an extended period of time, as Muybridge analyzed individual motions into successive stills. One of the inevitable results is the viewer's tendency to conceptually resynthesize these segments – as Muybridge resynthesized stills with the Zoopraxiscope – into a sense of the original continuity, even as we explore the implications of Sonbert's embedding each segment within a very particular context. In a general sense, *The Carriage Trade* is a grid. Although the many individual shots are not of precisely equal length, they are all relatively short; and the overall feeling of the film's organization is serial.

From its opening moments, *The Carriage Trade* demands an unconventional kind of viewer engagement. The first shots do not reveal any standard continuity, and, in fact, the precise nature of the interrelationships between shots is evident only after careful study. The film begins with a six-second shot of part of the front of a building, on the left, and its reflection in some sort of mirror, on the right – filmed, at a guess, in an Italian city (Rome and Venice are identifiable later in the film). After a partial fade-out and fade-in, we see a four-second shot of a narrow waterfall, flowing along pink rock from the upper right corner of the image to the lower left corner, bisecting the image. The scene is reminiscent of various locales in the Amer-

From New York to Turkey to Morocco in three successive shots from Warren Sonbert's *The Carriage Trade* (1973).

ican West, though the waterfall could also be somewhere in North Africa or in the Middle East, central locations in *The Carriage Trade*.

The juxtaposition of the two images can be read in several ways. The contrast of city and country is a preview of Sonbert's subsequent exploration of a wide range of urban and rural terrains and activities, and the distinction between a still, framed composition in which the only motion is the slight quiver of the hand-held camera, and an image in which something is moving through the frame foreshadows the wide variety of filming tactics used in *The Carriage Trade*. The fact that, within each image, space is graphically divided, by very different means, and that the diagonal motion of the waterfall echoes a diagonal wire that crosses the first image from the upper right center of the image to the lower left corner – and further, that the subtle jiggle of the hand-held camera in the second image echoes the even-more-subtle jiggle in the first image – begins a pattern of relationships-within-differences that is consistent throughout the film. On a conceptual level, each image suggests distinct, though complementary, metaphors for film as an art form. Film is, on one hand, a mirror – a reflection of and on life, *and* it is a flow of movement; it is, first (first, both literally and historically), concerned with framing and spatial composition, like the medium of still photography out of which it grew, and then, with editing, the flow of images, one after another, in time.

The opening pair of images is followed by a series of subtly related shots. The waterfall image fades out, and is replaced by a close-up of a television screen with just some interference lines moving vertically upward through the image. This somewhat longer shot (twelve seconds) is a surprise after the opening shots: it is very different in its emptiness (viewers see only that they aren't seeing a conventional image), in its implications of an indoor space, and in its color. And yet, the rhythmic upward flow of the white interference lines echoes the rhythmic motion of the waterfall. Immediately after the television image, a shot of part of a building front fades in, revealing (for six seconds) a doorway covered by a curtain behind the bottom of which a broom is sweeping in short horizontal motions that subtly echo the rhythms of the interference lines and the waterfall. To the left of the doorway there's a chicken in a cage and to the right of the doorway, inexplicably, an old wheelchair. The "mystery" of the empty television screen is echoed by the various "mysteries" within this image. A fade-out and fade-in reveals a street corner in an Arab town and a man selling postcards arranged on a vertical cylindrical stand. This postcard stand functions as a metaphor for *The Carriage Trade*, in which individual images of many places and many subjects are arranged next to one another on reels. If this implication is not clear by the fifth shot, it is certainly clear in the triad of images that follow: a long shot of a strange white landscape – just the sort of geological curiosity so many postcards market; a gorgeous shot of dramatic mottled shadows on multicolored building fronts recorded in Marrakech; and a shot of buildings, palm trees, and blue sky with fluffy clouds, framed like a postcard.

As *The Carriage Trade* develops, viewers' engagement with any particular type of visual development – whether it's a certain geographic location or a rhythm or direction of movement within an image – is inevitably interrupted, as Sonbert's editing shifts us to new locations. But shot by shot, sequence by sequence, Sonbert develops the myriad elements of his diverse images so that viewers can choose to be engaged not only in the visual and conceptual subtleties of his juxtapositions, but in an increasingly elaborate set of motifs. The more fully Sonbert's imagery is examined, the more pervasive the motif structure seems.

The motifs developed in *The Carriage Trade* include both what is filmed and how it is filmed. Periodically, the film focuses on particular kinds of places, activities, monuments, life forms, individual people, recorded in various countries on several continents. Sonbert films busy markets in many cities; parks in which children are playing; musicians making music; amusement parks. There is a set of famous landmarks – the Eiffel Tower, the Grand Canal and St. Mark's Square, the Taj Mahal, the Empire State Building, the Egyptian Sphinx – as well as sets of images of bridges, towers, bodies of water, outdoor food vendors, male/female and male/male couples, social rituals (weddings, acts of worship, parades – even a set of images of people eating cake), animals, birds, flowers, vehicles, boats. Each motif tends to be recognizable as a motif even though it might be recorded in a variety of ways: the Eiffel Tower, for example, is seen in black and white, as Sonbert circles it, taking a few frames at a time *and* in color, from an elevator ascending the tower.

Motifs can also be described in terms of dimensions of Sonbert's camerawork, composition, and other formal elements. There are sets of images filmed from various kinds of vehicles, including subsets filmed out the windows of airplanes, or on elevators; a set of images recorded upside down; a set of images during which Sonbert turns the camera 180°. There is a set of images filmed through circular shapes, arches, fences; and another set during which Sonbert circles people or monuments. There are also sets of images recorded in black and white; images recorded through monochromatic filters; images Sonbert has painted; images during which beginning- and end-of-roll flares are visible, a set of images that include at least one bright red detail. Finally, for those who are familiar with the films Sonbert made before *The Carriage Trade,* there is even a set of images recycled from previous films.

Within particular passages, the literal and/or conceptual direction of movement often becomes a motif. Early in the film, for example, a stream of water flowing through some sort of man-made watercourse, from the bottom foreground of the image into the distance is followed by a shot of a river flowing from the left side of the image into the distance, then by a vertical pan from a duck in a pond (the direction the duck moves echoes the direction of the water in the previous shot), then by another shot of the river during which a man slides over rocks with the left-flowing water; his leftward motion is picked up by a shot out the window of a plane taking off, and continued in a leftward camera movement over a flower garden. During another passage, back-and-forth movement becomes a motif. In the tenth shot an elephant sways back and forth. This back-and-forth motion is echoed seven shots later by the movement of a swing in a children's park, and, several shots after this, by a car stuck in the snow, rocking back and forth (this back-and-forth motion of the car creates a caesura of the leftward motion that develops in the sequence discussed a moment ago), then, conceptually, by the movement of people and vehicles in both directions past each other on a bridge in Istanbul, then by two men who are apparently handing a pipe back and forth...

Ultimately, any given image within *The Carriage Trade* becomes a nexus where various motifs intersect. One particular shot of the Arc de Triomphe, for example, includes several distinguishable motifs: It is a famous monument; it's a Parisian location (locations in Paris, filmed in many different ways, are interspersed throughout the film); it's a black-and-white image; and it's an instance of Sonbert's circling 360° around a subject. A brief shot of a snake charmer hypnotizing two cobras is a nexus for at least four motifs: The man's playing the flute is one of many outdoor performances of music; the snake charmer's swaying is a back-and-forth movement; the shot involves exotic animals; and the fact that there are two cobras ties the image into the film's extensive motif of couples. Literally every shot in *The Carriage Trade* can sustain this type of discussion, and, in some cases, the complexity is multiplied by Sonbert's decision to superimpose images (this happens more frequently during the second half of the film). I cannot imagine a viewing of *The Carriage Trade* during which even the most alert viewers could feel satisfied that they'd been aware of the wealth of connections built into the mammoth montage. Indeed, the feeling of not quite being able to grasp the suggestiveness of the images is one of the most consistent effects of the film.

One dimension of the immense montage of *The Carriage Trade* that distinguishes it from nearly all previous critical cinema is the implicit assumption that all sectors of the world, all peoples, have equal call on the filmmaker's and viewer's sensibilities and attention. In conventional films, changes of location usually require preparation and a clear transition: Often, intertexts identify the location where subsequent action will occur. And the more dramatic the change in location, the more extensive the cultural distinction between the original location and the destination, the more elaborate such preparation is. In *The Carriage Trade* there is no preparation at all for changing location, regardless of the extensiveness of the difference between the particular cultures recorded. Each straight cut is sure to locate viewers in a new geography (or return them to a geography previously visited), but the "distance" from one shot to the next can be across town or around the world.

Sonbert records imagery wherever he goes. His movement across national and cultural boundaries in *The Carriage Trade* – and in such films as *Divided Loyalties* (1978), *A Woman's Touch* (1983), *The Cup and the Lip* (1986), and *Friendly Witness* (1989) – is not a function of a particular commitment to the use of cinema to "internationalize" the world. Rather, it is a reflection of Sonbert's assumption that, for a film artist, national boundaries and other political "realities" are relevant only to the degree to which they enable or constrict the artistic process. And yet, his approach implicitly demonstrates a politic that subverts a cinematic convention.

Most commercial films in which protagonists travel, and most other kinds of film in which travel is a central issue, assume a home, a privileged place, from which one comes and to which one must return. The places visited are, by definition, something *else,* exotic locales interesting fundamentally as contrasts to the traveler's (and viewer's) norms, which will send the traveler home, rewarded, "enlightened," and satisfied. There is no privileged place in *The Carriage Trade.* Not only do we not leave from and return to an identifiable home or homeland, we cannot even be sure where exactly we are, except during those moments when Sonbert films famous monuments and immediately recognizable scenes. In *The Carriage Trade* all places are equally exotic; the camera seems no more intimate with one location than with another. It's true that Sonbert travels to some locations (Paris, Venice) that are tourist stops for many North Americans, but these places draw visitors from many sectors of the globe. A North African watching the film might well recognize as many of the locations recorded as an American, but they would be somewhat different locations. For Sonbert all people and places are equally "filmic": All are sources of imagery that is interesting to filmically explore and to recontextualize.

In *The Carriage Trade,* home is the perceptual/conceptual space that develops as Sonbert discovers in the imagery he's recorded those elements with which he will build a visual structure. Of course, the basic technology he uses – a hand-held 16mm camera – and the film tradition of which *The Carriage Trade* is a recognizable instance must be counted among these elements, and to a degree they do identify Sonbert's filmmaking practice as part of a particular, Western cultural enterprise. Nevertheless, Sonbert's particular approach to filmic structure seems a good deal less narrowly defined than the conventions of commercial cinema.

As a finished film, *The Carriage Trade* has the potential to function within the larger world in a manner analogous to the way each individual shot within the film functions within Sonbert's overall structure. The huge montage provides viewers with a cinematic space for perceptual and conceptual exploration. Since the film's structure is built of visual qualities of shape, movement, and color that any viewer can perceive, and since even the moments of human activity that form most of the motifs are generally abstracted from the specifics of their particular cultural surrounds (even the recognizable landmarks are often decontextualized, by Sonbert's ways of recording), *The Carriage Trade* becomes a cinematic nexus where people from a variety of geographic and historical circumstances might meet. No particular individual's reading of the montage could be any more or less correct than any other's. Indeed, any new reading could only elaborate the implications of the film's particulars in ways that confirm their perceptual and conceptual fertility and the film's general openness.

In its overall structure and shot-by-shot articulation, *The Carriage Trade* confronts the closed structures of conventional films, where each image has a particular definable part to play in each film's relentless march toward a reconfirmation of the viewer's culture-bound expectations and of the ideology that underlies them – and in a return on the producer's investment. That Sonbert has chosen the montage form is particularly appropriate, given the cultural history of montage since it was developed by the Soviets in the 1920s. For Eisenstein the montage became a way of achieving the maximum intensification of dialectic principles, and he exploited it brilliantly. But, for all its ingenuity of conception and articulation, and despite the revolutionary idealism out of which it developed, Soviet montage – especially as epitomized by Eisenstein in *Potemkin* – has been relentlessly coopted not only by the commercial cinema, but by television advertising. Indeed, the traditional structure of the American television hour – slower-paced narrative building toward a bombardment of dialectically arranged images in a series of advertisements – is, for all practical purposes, modeled on Eisensteinian principles. In the contemporary capitalist exploitations of the Soviet breakthroughs in editing, the montage has become the fullest intensification of precisely the opposite goals for which it was developed.

For Sonbert, however, the *cinematic* ideologies of the Soviet films of the 1920s and of contemporary television advertising are more similar than different: Both attempt to coerce viewers into particular forms of action. Sonbert critiques this parallel by creating a film form that implies no preconceived goal other than the experience of the film. By decontextualizing his montage from any particular political or economic system, Sonbert has created a cinematic, cross-cultural no-man's-land in which almost any film viewer can find a place.

Street scene in Morocco, from *The Carriage Trade.*

1. Sonbert in "Point of View," *Spiral,* no. 1 (October 1984), pp. 4, 5. The best source of information about Sonbert's work is *Film Culture,* nos. 70–1 (1983), which includes a special Sonbert section.

2. The title is a pun: Sonbert does include images of people who fit the conventional meaning of the phrase – wealthy patrons of a restaurant or of the theater – but "carriage" also refers to the many vehicles Sonbert films and films from. There may also be a somewhat ironic suggestion that while the arts have conventionally been a central interest of the carriage trade, Sonbert's film art is more humble.

12
Godfrey Reggio
Powaqqatsi

Whereas the internationalism of *The Carriage Trade* was less Sonbert's goal than a by-product of travels he took for other reasons, the internationalism of Godfrey Reggio's *Powaqqatsi* was of primary concern. Indeed, the implicit journeys documented in Reggio's second feature were as fully a means of articulating his worldview as Luca Comerio's journeys were a function of his Italian nationalism. And, although Reggio's attitudes are very different from Comerio's, his cinematic means for articulating them suggest a return to the original cinematic fascination with studying the motions of the exotic that motivated Comerio, a fascination embodied first in much of the work of Muybridge and the Lumières.

In this volume, I have dealt with the influence of Muybridge and the Lumières as if their approaches to visual imagery ceased to be important for mass audiences once conventional narrative came to dominate the commercial industry – on the assumption that it is precisely the fact that their approaches *were* left behind that made them useful for critical filmmakers decades later. And yet, in at least one sense, this is a distortion. Although the hunger for extended narrative came to dominate the desire of film audiences, other interests – including the interests that presumably led audiences to Muybridge's lectures with the Zoopraxiscope and to the early Lumière shows – have continued to play a crucial role in certain sectors of conventional mass entertainment, specifically in the world of specialty screening rooms so central to World's Fairs, theme parks, and big-city tourist areas: 360° movies, Naturemax, Omnimax, and so on. In these cine-extravaganzas, the magic that early viewers must have felt at seeing Muybridge's resynthesized one-second movies and the Lumières' projections of everyday and exotic imagery is still very much in evidence.

Godfrey Reggio is one of the few American filmmakers I am aware of

who has managed to use methods familiar from this area of film experience for a cultural and cinematic critique that has attracted a feature-film audience of considerable size. He has done it twice, with *Koyaanisqatsi* (1983) and *Powaqqatsi* (1988), and is working on a third film, *Naqoyqatsi* (the titles are variations on the Hopi word *qatsi*, meaning life), which will complete what he considers a trilogy.[1] Whereas nearly all the filmmakers discussed in this volume have assumed that their commitment to critical cinema means their audiences will be comparatively small, Reggio and his financial collaborators have been confident enough that he can attract sizable audiences that he has worked exclusively in 35mm.

Until he was twenty-eight, Reggio lived an ascetic life, as part of a strict religious community. This unusual background helps to account for the unconventional approaches of his two films, and it seems to have prepared the way for the mixture of extravagant visual sensuality and moral seriousness that characterizes *Koyaanisqatsi* and *Powaqqatsi*. Of the two films, *Koyaanisqatsi* has been more financially successful. Indeed, its popularity is something of a phenomenon, given the unconventionality of the film's style and structure. *Koyaanisqatsi* provides a visual interpretation of contemporary American life, though only financial limitations prevented Reggio from extending his interpretation to other sectors of the industrialized world – Europe and Japan, in particular. The film's frequently stunning visuals are accompanied – as is *Powaqqatsi* – by Philip Glass music. The power of Reggio's imagery is a function not so much of his subject matter, but of the way in which the imagery is presented. Nothing in *Koyaanisqatsi* is presented "normally," that is, within the range of normal-motion medium shots, long shots, and close-ups that characterize most filmmaking (including most documentary). Reggio's primary techniques are time-lapse and aerial photography.[2]

In general, these techniques are crucial for Reggio because they make possible a critique of American culture *and* of the conventional cinematic depiction of it:

> This sounds very simplistic, but one of the obvious things I noticed was that in most films the foreground was where the plot and characterization took place, where the screenplay came in, and how you directed the photography. Everything was foreground; background (music included) basically supported characterization and plot. So

Images of India (*top*) and Egypt (*middle and bottom*), from Godfrey Reggio's *Powaqqatsi* (1988).

what I did was to try to eradicate all of the foreground of traditional film and take the background, or what's called "second unit," and make *that* foreground, give *that* the principal focus. We were trying to look at buildings, masses of people, transportation, industrialization, as autonomous *entities*. Same thing with Nature: Rather than seeing Nature as something dead, something inorganic like a stone, we wanted to see it as having its own life form, unanthropomorphized, unrelated to human beings, here for billions of years before human beings arrived on the planet, having its own entity. That's what I tried to put into the film; what people get out of it is another matter. I was trying to show in Nature the presence of a life form, an entity, a beingness; and in the synthetic world the presence of a different entity, a consuming and inhuman entity.[3]

At the conclusion of *Koyaanisqatsi*, its polemical edge is made quite explicit, when Reggio reveals the meaning of his title – "*ko yaa nis qatsi* (from the Hopi language) n. 1. crazy life. 2. life in turmoil. 3. life out of balance. 4. life disintegrating. 5. a state of life that calls for another way of living" – and translates three Hopi prophecies: "If we dig precious things from the land, we will invite disaster"; "Near the Day of Purification, there will be cobwebs spun back and forth across the sky"; "A container of ashes might one day be thrown from the sky, which could burn the land and boil the oceans." It can be argued that the pleasure we take in the magic of Reggio's imagery overwhelms and undercuts the film's polemic, and leaves us with the irony of Reggio's use of an unusually technologically oriented cinematic strategy to produce a warning about the dangers of modern technology – a warning whose most noticeable impact on modern life has been to provide advertisers with new stylistic gestures for selling assembly-line products. But Reggio is fully aware of this paradox:

the film is using as high a base of technology as was possible at the time. That consideration lost me money and got me accused of being hypocritical, confused. I don't see it that way. If I could have immaculately presented my point of view by *thinking about it*, then I would have done so and saved myself the effort. Obviously, that's impossible: no Immaculate Conception is taking place. I felt that I had to embrace the contradiction and walk on the edge, use the very tools I was criticizing to make the statement I was making – knowing that people learn in terms of what they already know. In that sense, I saw myself, if I may be so bold, as a cultural kamikaze, as a Trojan horse, using the coinage of the time in order to raise a question about that very coinage.[4]

While the subject of *Koyaanisqatsi* is modern technological society, the subject of its companion piece, *Powaqqatsi,* is the Third World. Sequences were shot in multiple locations in each of seven nations (Peru, Brazil, Kenya, Egypt, Hong Kong, Nepal, India), as well as in Jerusalem, Berlin, and Chartres. Reggio took a crew to each location and hired local people as grips, drivers, and assistants. Although the production process was similar to that used for conventional films shot in Third World locations, the subject and Reggio's handling of it are quite unconventional. In mass-market movies the Third World is at most a decorative backdrop for the adventures of First World characters. Here the Third World *is* the central subject matter; the audience is confronted with those very sectors of the world and those activities that, in the popular mind, are precisely what one goes to the movies *not* to see or think about.

Whereas *Koyaanisqatsi* centers on time-lapse fast motion that captures the frenzy of modern, industrialized life, *Powaqqatsi* uses slow motion almost exclusively, often combining it with aerial and telephoto shooting in order to sing the dignity of life in the less-industrialized Southern Hemisphere. *Powaqqatsi* begins with a six-minute prologue that sets the tone and provides a stunning, multileveled metaphor. Hundreds of men are carrying dirt out of a huge open mine. With few exceptions, the shots are close-ups, filmed in extreme slow motion – not so extreme as in Ono's early films, but slow enough so that, in the opening sequence, the men look like classic sculptures and their movements like dance. On one level, the workers are reminiscent of the Greek mythic figure of Sisyphus, but the concluding image of a man being carried out of the mine adds a different, but related, metaphor: The position of the man's body is reminiscent of the Crucifixion and the Pietà, and, as a result, the shot suggests the systematic "crucifixion" of labor. The mood of the sequence is complex: Viewers may feel sorry for these hard-working men, but, at the same time, their strength and persistence is impressive, even exhilarating: They are beautiful to watch. And there is a timelessness to the opening sequence that enhances its metaphoric implications. The kind of labor we are watching has been part of human societies for millennia. In fact, it continues to be a part of what makes *our* lives possible.

The pre-credit sequence ends with a brief, highly energized montage of shots taken from airplanes or helicopters moving forward, low-to-the-ground over various landscapes, a visual tactic that broadens the implications of the labor documented in the opening montage and delivers viewers to an image of superimposed, revolving faces (a metaphor for the many related "faces" of everyday life in the Southern Hemisphere that will be documented by the film) and to the title, which is as mysterious as "Koyaanisqatsi": The definition of *powaqqatsi* is not provided until the end of the film. After the titles, Reggio moves from one unidentified location to another, presenting consistently remarkable slow-motion imagery. At least as clearly as any film discussed in this volume, *Powaqqatsi* combines an interest in (Muybridgian) motion study and (Lumièresque) meditation.[5] Whereas conventional cinema relentlessly ignores the fact and implications of physical labor, Reggio's combination of slow motion and extended shots allows for a contemplation of the variety and beauty of individual, laboring human beings. Almost immediately following the title, Reggio presents a fifty-two-second shot of two women carrying huge bundles on their heads, walking quickly along a road in the early morning mist. The Glass accompaniment emphasizes the grace of the movements, which have the impact of a miraculous dance. *Powaqqatsi* is regularly punctuated by such imagery.

Many of the most memorable individual shots in *Powaqqatsi* concern children. Early in the film, an eighty-seven-second close-up tracking shot pans across the faces of dozens of African children: Their faces and their varied reactions to the camera are lovely and compelling. Several minutes later, another forty-seven-second close-up tracking shot past other children's faces echoes the first. The myriad physical and psychological differences among the children recorded in these shots offer a critique of the conventional cinema's frequent use of Third World characters as types, as representatives of unindividuated masses. This critique is extended by the shots of individual children so frequent in *Powaqqatsi*, shots that allow viewers to contemplate the children and their circumstances, and, in some cases, the way these children respond to being observed. One of the most electrifying shots in *Powaqqatsi* – actually the first of two related shots – is a close-up of a young child driving a horse-drawn wagon in the midst of heavy city traffic, while a man lies asleep on the seat next to him. The density of the fast-moving traffic and the tiny child relentlessly pounding the horses with a stick to keep their speed up creates an epiphany of the young age at which some of the world's children must learn to function as adults. A similar idea is conveyed by a continuous slow-motion shot of a tiny child walking along a highway toward the camera. The shot is divided into two halves so that during the first half, a huge truck moves toward the child from behind; at first, it appears as if the truck will hit the child, and, when it does finally pass him, the child disappears in a cloud of dust. The shot seems to end. But, after other imagery has intervened and most viewers have probably understood the child's disappearance as a metaphor for the destruction of childhood by the circumstances of industrialization, Reggio returns to the shot: The thick dust disperses and the child emerges, not only unscathed, but seemingly unaware that anything unusual has occurred. The shot is transformed into a metaphor for the strength and resilience of Third World children, and for their ability to surprise our assumptions about them.

The gaze of some of the children back at the camera (and by implication at us) adds to the impact of the film. During one sixty-five-second shot, a tiny girl walks along a sidewalk. The camera is set up so that the girl is seen from the opposite side of the street in front of a wall on which graffiti announces, "*Viva la guerra de guerrillas.*" The poignancy of the tiny child growing up not only on the streets of a busy city, but in the midst of dangerous political developments, makes the shot powerful. But the fact of the child's open confrontation of the camera during much of the shot suggests a sense of inner strength and clarity, and an openness to experience that render her more than "an innocent victim": She is a person going about her business, and curious about the world. This shot echoes a twenty-six-second, slow-motion shot of a young, naked black boy walking in the surf.

Plane landing over Hong Kong, from the 35mm *Powaqqatsi*.

143

During most of the shot he seems unaware that he is being observed, but then he looks toward the camera, curious but undeterred from his walk, as if to confront our assumption of visual omniscience.

The imagery in *Powaqqatsi* is arranged in an overall montage, punctuated by sequences that explore particular themes. Like *The Carriage Trade*, *Powaqqatsi* can be understood as a critique of conventional uses of montage, though the nature of the critique here is quite different. Whereas Sonbert removes montage from its usual position as an intensifier of ideology, Reggio maintains its function vis-à-vis ideology, but alters its usual pace. Generally, the editing in a montage moves much more quickly than the editing in the sequences around it. Indeed, this greater frequency of editing is part of the standard definition of a montage. But, whereas conventional montages, particularly in their pervasive use in television advertising, function to polemicize greater levels of consumption (of products, of film images per minute), Reggio's montage is as fully slow motion as his individual images. It demands that we foreswear normal consumption patterns and meditate on individual human beings in those sectors of the world that are being transformed economically and politically by the patterns of consumption and activity we and others like us have set in motion – the patterns revealed by Reggio's time-lapse imagery in *Koyaanisqatsi*.

In general, the overall montage of *Powaqqatsi* begins with rural life and ends in cities, though the contrast here is not, as it is in *Koyaanisqatsi*, between the natural environment, unmediated by human beings, and human society. *Powaqqatsi* provides a panorama of environments within which people are living. In addition to Reggio's primary focus on physical labor, there are sequences devoted to spiritual life, to children playing, to people dancing, to the miraculous ways in which people live in harmony with the environment, and even much of the imagery of city life seems primarily involved with singing the variety of the world – especially those segments of the world the conventional cinema reveals, at most, only in passing. The overall trajectory in *Powaqqatsi* is from grueling rural labor to the increasingly frenzied life in the cities. But, as hard as the country people work, transporting things on their backs or on boats, threshing grain, and doing other physical tasks, their labors seem more dignified, more beautiful, than the efforts of the harried city people to make a place for themselves. Even though nearly the entire film is in slow motion, in the cities the frame is often so dense with people and vehicles that the slowed pace of the imagery merely emphasizes the relentless congestion. That the situation in the Southern Hemisphere is deteriorating is confirmed by Reggio's superimposing one congested city shot on another near the end of the film.

The body of the film ends with the title, in red, and the definition: *"pow waq qat si* (from the Hopi language, *powaq* sorcerer + *qatsi* life) n. an entity, a way of life, that consumes the life forces of other beings in order to further its own life." The definition seems calculated to confirm the Marxist implications of Reggio's decision to devote *Powaqqatsi* to imagery of the Third World, and to begin the film with a sequence that suggests the exploitation of Third World labor by economic forces. But the film is not a call for immediate revolution, the way *Potemkin* is often assumed to be. The fascination with individuals at work revealed by Reggio's meditative slow-motion imagery asks not that Marxists or capitalists come to the rescue, but that those people in societies that support the types of industrial structures that have produced and maintained the commercial cinema – that is, those of us who have access to this film – use this technology as a way of making contact with the beauty and meaning of valuable forms of human adaptation to the natural world that are increasingly endangered by industrial systems, in both Marxist and capitalist nations, by the relentless spread of consumer culture.

The paradox of *Koyaanisqatsi* – the fact that the problems of modern technology are presented in a quintessentially technological medium – is reframed in *Powaqqatsi:* Reggio uses film technology to exploit Third World individuals in order to argue that industrial exploitation is dangerous to their lives and cultures. Viewers of many persuasions may want Reggio to supply them with a political "escape" – a feeling that the problems of Third World countries are decried and positioned within an ideological framework that allows us to feel horror without complicity, that enables us to feel part of a system that is "improving" the conditions we see. But the film offers no such escape:

> These films are based on the premise that the question is the mother of the answer. There's no attempt to provide an answer. First of all, giving people answers does them no service; I found out as a pedagogue that the intrinsic principle of learning is the *learner,* not the teacher. All the teacher can do is set the environment. . . . I'm hoping that people can let go of themselves, forget about time, and become mesmerized by the experience. Once the experience is had, and held, which is certainly not going to happen for everyone . . . *then* the process of reflection can start to take place.[6]

"Powaqqatsi" is as much a comment on the cinematic experience itself as on politics. In a traditional filmic sense, after all, Reggio is a "sorcerer." His use of slow-motion, aerial, and telephoto photography (and, in *Ko-*

yaanisqatsi, time-lapse) ties him historically to Georges Méliès's transformation of stage magic into the "trick film." And filmmaking in general is a way of life that "consumes the life forces of other beings in order to further its own life." Reggio's trick has been to transform people who usually function as a decorative backdrop to the antics of macho Western "individuals" into the foreground and focus of a feature film. He has been able to explore his fascination with film technology and stay economically viable as a 35mm filmmaker without ignoring the majority of the world, the way Western commercial cinema consistently has done and the way the economically disadvantaged critical cinema has often had to do.

NOTES

1. One notable American predecessor of *Koyaanisqatsi* in particular is Ralph Steiner and Willard Van Dyke's *The City*, an experimental documentary produced for the 1939 World's Fair, where it was a popular favorite. In structure and ideology, *The City* is closely related to *Koyaanisqatsi*, though its technical means are different.
2. Time-lapse has a considerable history in avant-garde film. Indeed, several American films from recent decades seem particularly relevant to a discussion of *Koyaanisqatsi*. In 1964, Marie Menken finished *Go Go Go*, a portrait of New York City life that includes lovely time-lapse passages of New York harbor: ferries, tugs, even ocean liners scoot across the water like water bugs. In 1975 Hilary Harris finished *Organism*, a twenty-minute film that intercuts between blood flowing through arteries and veins and time-lapse imagery of traffic moving along the "arteries" of New York City. Harris, who has a credit on *Koyaanisqatsi*, uses the motion-study potential of time-lapse to demonstrate the idea that external reality as created and developed by humans is, fundamentally, a projection of internal physical systems. Another recent experiment with time lapse, used in particular to study New York City life, is Peter von Ziegesar's *Concern for the City* (1986). The avant-garde filmmaker who has probably done the most to demonstrate the potential of time-lapse is Toronto Super-8mm filmmaker John Porter, who has explored the technique in the series of films he calls *Porter's Condensed Rituals*.
3. Interview with Reggio in Scott MacDonald, *A Critical Cinema 2* (Berkeley, CA: University of California Press, 1992), p. 390.
4. *A Critical Cinema 2*, pp. 390–1.
5. One seventy-seven-second, slow motion, telephoto shot of a crowded commuter train recalls the Lumières' *L'Arrivée du train en gare*.
6. *A Critical Cinema 2*, p. 391.

I3
Trinh T. Minh-ha
Naked Spaces – Living Is Round

Trinh T. Minh-ha's interest in using film to question the cultural narrowness of most commercial cinema developed in large measure out of the opportunities her status as a Vietnamese exile has given her to observe the way in which people in industrialized societies view other cultural groups. Unlike Reggio, who seems particularly concerned with Western consumer culture and its embodiment in commercial film, Trinh's critique of convention has been consistently relevant not only to the popular cinema's depiction of other cultures, but to the tradition of ethnographic documentary, which has generally been seen – and has seen itself – as a corrective to the distortions of the industry. Ethnographic filmmakers have often made long and dangerous journeys to remote sectors of the globe to document and interpret those nonliterate cultural groups that have been affected least by the forces of large-state imperialism, industrialization, and modern technology. The resulting films almost inevitably critique the conventional cinema's crude depictions of "primitive" peoples as decorations for the adventures of heroes, as sources of comedy and terror, and as exotic auras for conventionalized notions of romance; and they recognize these peoples for their remarkable achievements in coming to terms with their environments.

The fact that the history of ethnographic film has provided a critique of the conventional cinema's exploitation of indigenous peoples has been less important for Trinh than what ethnographic film has shared with the commercial cinema. For her, this critical tradition, as well as the commercial cinema, is itself in need of critique. Of course, well before Trinh made *Reassemblage* (1982), ethnographic filmmakers had been turning a critical eye on the films of those who had preceded them and on their own work. Timothy Asch and Napoleon Chagnon's *Ax Fight* (1975), for instance, is, in large measure, about the dangers of first impressions, even on the part

147

of anthropologists who have spent substantial portions of their lives in the field. The Asch–Chagnon film begins with Chagnon misinterpreting an ax fight in a Yanomamo village; and the subsequent sections of the film demonstrate that ethnology and ethnographic filmmaking can be processes of refining the truth of what is recorded on film: Asch and Chagnon re-present and reinterpret their original, candid footage of the ax fight several times. Their decision to make this process evident in a finished work was a response to an earlier tendency of filmmakers to present what they felt they knew about indigenous peoples·from an apparently omniscient perspective – a tendency that has been increasingly recognized as problematic.

For Trinh, however, the limitations of the traditional ethnographic film are merely instances of a general tendency in industrialized nations to patronize the experiences of other societies, a tendency she experienced and observed in Vietnam during the American presence there, as a Vietnamese immigrant to the United States and France (she left Vietnam in 1970), and, subsequently, during the years (1977–80) she lived and worked in Senegal. *Reassemblage* (1982) and *Naked Spaces – Living Is Round* (1985) are responses to this tendency, as it is embodied in the cinematic representation of African peoples.

Nearly every dimension of *Reassemblage* can be understood as critique, either of ethnographic film in particular or of the history of film in general. Many ethnographic films have a carefully defined focus, a particular subject to be documented and interpreted as precisely as possible. *Reassemblage* not only has no specific topic – no single person viewers get to know, no single artifact, or event, or activity, or ritual – Trinh is open about her decision precisely *not* to choose a particular topic for analysis: On the soundtrack, she says, "A film about what? my friends ask./A film about Senegal; but what in Senegal?"[1] What is seen and heard during the forty minutes of *Reassemblage* is an immense image/sound montage that records various dimensions of everyday domestic life within several rural Senegalese villages in hundreds of brief shots (most are less than three seconds long; shots longer than ten seconds are rare): There are women hoeing, turning grain into food, taking care of children and of themselves, dancing, and interacting; children playing, eating, sleeping; and, less frequently, men weaving baskets and clothes. In addition to Trinh's narration, the soundtrack includes women singing, music accompanying dances, the sounds of

West African scenes from Trinh T. Minh-ha's *Naked Spaces – Living Is Round* (1985).

domestic labor (often difficult to distinguish from music), and a variety of natural sounds.

The focus on women and children in *Reassemblage* is one of the primary dimensions of its critique of cinematic depictions of non-Western peoples: of commercial adventure films, which focus on men and use white women as romantic/erotic interest (women of color rarely play any significant role); and of traditional ethnographic film, which has often focused on male activities, and particularly those activities that are the focus of many commercial adventure films – large- and small-scale battles, confrontations of Man and Nature. Trinh's exploration of domestic life is an inversion of conventional film expectations shared by commercial and academic audiences alike – an inversion which, by breaking the "rules" of cinematic representation, puts viewers more in touch with the realities of Senegalese life, or, to be more precise, in touch with an interplay between Trinh and particular communities of West Africans.

Many of the ideas and procedures central to *Reassemblage*, as well as Senegal as a subject, were again central in *Naked Spaces – Living Is Round*. In the later film, however, the geographic scope of Trinh's interest is greatly expanded and this expanded scope is reconfirmed in the new film's greater length (135 minutes) and more serene pace. *Naked Spaces – Living Is Round* begins and ends in Senegal, but also transports viewers to other West African nations. Overall, the film breaks into seven sections of varying lengths. The first Senegalese section (20 minutes) is followed by 20-minute Mauritania and Togo sections, then by Mali (10 minutes), Burkina Faso (23¾ minutes), Benin (5¾ minutes), and by the long final Senegalese section (34 minutes). Changes of location in the visuals from one nation to the next and from one community to another within a particular country are indicated textually. While the dense montage of *Reassemblage* is reminiscent of the Soviet use of montage in the political polemics of the twenties, *Naked Spaces – Living Is Round* allows viewers to explore village life at greater leisure.

Each of the longer sections divides into subsections focusing on various villages. During her filming of each village and in her subsequent editing, Trinh was at pains to position herself, as she puts it in *Reassemblage*, not as "an objective observer," not as a person filmically "speaking about," but as a person who speaks "near by." The majority of the shots in *Naked Spaces – Living Is Round* are pans. These pans are unusual – consistently so. They have neither the goal-orientation of conventional Hollywood panning, which relentlessly moves us toward a preconceived visual point that fits neatly into the developing narrative, nor the personal expressiveness of Stan Brakhage's gestural camera movements. Trinh's pans are consistently halting. They start and stop and start in a manner that makes clear that Trinh does not mean to focus us on any one detail, or to provide the "best" view, the "correct" perspective on a scene. The pans move horizontally and/ or vertically across sectors of village life, allowing viewers to see as much as they can – and to draw their own conclusions about what to take note of in any given image. The film image becomes a visual and conceptual intersection of African activities, artifacts and cultural forms *and* those of a very different culture, where making a film is considered a meaningful activity. Trinh continually confronts the tendency of Western filmgoers and filmmakers (including some ethnographic filmmakers) to see the camera as a neutral technology capable of providing an objective view of experience. The unconventionality of Trinh's stance in relation to the people she films is announced in the opening credits, which indicate that the film was "DIRECTED, PHOTOGRAPHED, WRITTEN, MUSIC RECORDED BY" Trinh T. Minh-ha, though "DIRECTED" is covered by a large X, suggesting that Trinh did not control the activities and places she filmed in a conventional directorial sense.

The film's imagery divides between shots made outdoors and shots made indoors: Nearly every passage alternates between inside and out, even when inside spaces are not, in a conventional film sense, well-lighted. Trinh's decision to film in low-light conditions is a reaction both to the Hollywood norm, where visual clarity is the rule and "darkness" is almost inevitably a pretext for suspense, violence, comedy, or sexuality – where darkness is always a problem or an excitement, rather than an ordinary and acceptable dimension of everyday perception – and to efforts in ethnographic film to "make clear" elements of other cultures that are subtle, ambiguous, shadowy. (One is reminded of Robert Flaherty's decision to reveal Nanook and family "waking up inside the igloo," by building a fake igloo with no top so that activities that occur in the shadows could be lit by the sun and become more practically filmic: we "see" what the Inuit do every morning, but because we see it as *we* perceive reality, rather than as Nanook and the others do, the Inuits' own experience is essentially decontextualized and patronized.)

Trinh's careful alternation between indoor and outdoor shooting also allows viewers to experience some of the visual subtleties in what the Africans see every day. Trinh frequently films from inside a dwelling, framing the image – or composing the pan – so that a sector of the bright world outside is seen through a door or window opening. In many cases, the space delimited by the doorway of the dwelling from within which the camera is filming reveals the doorway of a second dwelling across the way that frames the movements of someone inside. These shots may suggest that when the Africans sit inside and look out, their experience is a kind of cinema. Ironically, since our everyday experience is relentlessly lighted, we need to use complex technology to have an analogous experience. As we sit in the darkness of the theater looking through the "window" of the film image at "outdoor" scenes or into "private" spaces, we are participating in a modern version of an experience inevitable for peoples living in the types of dwellings Trinh is recording.

Although Trinh's use of darkness may reveal a dimension of the cultures she visits, it certainly does suggest her own experiences as visitor:

> When you walk from outside to the inside of most rural African houses, you come from a very bright sunlight to a very dark space where for a moment, you are totally blind. It takes some time to get adjusted to the darkness inside. This experience is one of the conceptual bases of *Naked Spaces*. To move inside oneself, one has to be willing to go intermittently blind. Similarly, to move toward other people, one has to take the jump and move ahead blindly at certain moments of inquiry. If one is not even momentarily blind, if one remains as one is from the outside or from the inside, then it is unlikely that one can break through that moment where suddenly everything stops, one's luggage is emptied out, and one moves in a state of non-knowningness, where destabilizing encounters with the "unfamiliar" or "unknown" are multiplied and experienced anew.[2]

Trinh's assumption that her own process as looker is as much her subject as what she views distinguishes *Naked Spaces* from *The Carriage Trade* and *Powaqqatsi*. As filmmaker Sonbert is less interested in the various Western and non-Western cultures he records than in the particular images he collects and what he can make from them. Reggio is conscious of the paradox of his use of high technology to document its dangers, but does not provide any reflection on his activities as a director in the process of examining others. Indeed, his particular choice of telephoto and aerial shooting implicitly undercuts the moments of "contact" that seem to occur when people look at the camera. As a result, in both *The Carriage Trade* and *Powaqqatsi*, nonindustrialized peoples tend to become as distant and/or romantic as they are in many commercial films. Trinh doesn't provide even the illusion of personal contact, but, by foregrounding her own process, she implicitly democratizes the camera's look: We view her and her African hosts viewing each other, or, as she puts it in *Reassemblage*, She is "looking through a circle [the camera lens] at a circle of looks."

The overall structure of *Naked Spaces* has a multileveled Muybridgian quality: The rectangular film frame, and Trinh's consistently horizontal and vertical pans, create a spatial grid within which viewers examine each village, *and* the structure of each village functions as a standard – a "grid" – against which viewers measure the filmmaker's movements; the filmmaker helps viewers see the village and vice versa. On a more general level, the film's movement from one village to another, from one country to another – using roughly the same filmic style in exploring each place – is an approach reminiscent of Muybridge: It makes possible a comparison of one variation on village life to another. The fact that the variations in villages are immense – there are grass huts, adobe villages, cliff houses, villages on water – can be understood as a corrective to the tendency of filmmakers in industrialized societies to see the variations among groups and individuals living in their own societies as significant and meaningful, but to act as though the variations in other, "less developed" areas of the world are not important or interesting.

The geographic region traversed in *Naked Spaces – Living Is Round* is roughly the size of Europe, but the Western tendency has been to think of

An African dwelling, from *Naked Spaces – Living Is Round.*

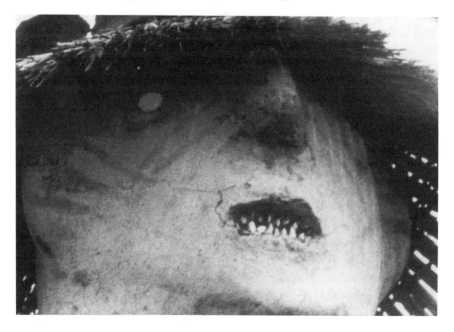

153

(and cinematically experience) Africa as a single place – or perhaps three: Moslem North Africa, Black Central Africa, and Apartheid South Africa – rather than as a set of cultural variations as extensive, complex, and worthy of note as those that make up Europe. By moving from one place to another within a region represented simplistically in those entertainment films that deign to admit the region exists at all, and in ethnographic films that isolate a single group within a single culture for extended investigation and often ignore the complex cultural surround that conditions the life of this small group, Trinh implicitly demonstrates that "global cinema" should not simply be a process of seeing the world as a global village, joined together by technologies exported by industrialized nations: It should expand our sense of the cultural diversity and accomplishments in those regions ideologically "miniaturized" by industrial societies.

Although the visuals are rigorously organized according to geographic locale, the soundtrack is not. As in *Reassemblage,* Trinh alternates between moments of silence, passages of local music and other environmental sounds, and narration. In *Naked Spaces – Living Is Round,* however, there are three narrative voices, each with a different function, as Trinh made explicit when she published the complete text of the narration in *Cinematograph* (Vol. 3, 1988): "Text written for three women's voices . . . : the low voice [Barbara Christian] . . . the only one that can sound assertive, remains close to the villagers' sayings and statements, and quotes African writers' works. The high-range voice [Linda Peckham] . . . informs according to Western logic and mainly quotes Western thinkers. The medium range voice [Trinh's] . . . speaks in the first person and relates personal feelings and observations."

Trinh's use of three voices, all of them women, confronts the conventional expectation of a single (male) narrative voice, speaking in an educated, mainstream Western tongue, that tends to wrap the foreign culture in a Western linguistic frame, just as the rectangular film frame and conventional camerawork enclose the culture within a visual context that is a product of Western logic and technology. The three female voices are very different not only in pitch but in accent. The voice closest to the filmmaker's direct responses to her travels – that is, the voice functioning most conventionally – is Trinh's; her Vietnamese accent, however, undercuts the convention: We know we are hearing one non-Western culture being described by a person from another non-Western culture. The other voices also have accents and vocal deliveries unconventional for documentary. Together, they create a chorus that is less a conventional explanation of the cultures we see – though insights of various kinds are included – than a dramatization of Trinh's recognition that the cultures an outside observer visits are always

experienced, by whoever experiences them, from within a continual surround of immediate perception and previously internalized wisdom (or "wisdom") from both women and men (while only women narrate, they
frequently quote statements by men), and from both local and extralocal
sources.

In general, the soundtrack is scored so that each type of sound (including
silent pauses between sounds) becomes a motif and so that different kinds
of sound and imagery periodically intersect. Although almost none of the
finished film is synchronized sound, each of the three narrators is in some
instances more fully "in sync" with the general subject matter of the visuals
than in others. By and large, the weave of sounds, and of sound and image,
is consistent through the film, though there are exceptions: The soundtrack
during the Benin section, for example, is entirely made up of counterpointed
voices. The overall organization of the soundtrack is musical: An implicit
critique of the tendency of ethnographic films, and commercial travel films
or documentaries on foreign cultures, to assume that a straightforward,
obvious relationship of sound and image is truest to reality.

Although Trinh's use of a roughly serial structure for both soundtrack
and visuals is reminiscent of Muybridge – at least as I've been using him
in this volume – Trinh's evocation of systematic organization functions not
as an acceptance of a systematic approach to the examination of culture,
but as an indication that she, like Su Friedrich, has *refused* rigorously systematic means. In fact, the Muybridge approach to gathering information
about human beings and animals can serve as a perfect metaphor for what
Naked Spaces is most centrally against. Muybridge's assumption that he
could learn about human movement by asking people to undress and move
in front of a linear grid has had considerable long-term impact on modern
life, not only because of his importance in the development of cinema, but
because of the appropriation of his methods by the generation of efficiency
experts who helped American industrialists refine the assembly line. Nevertheless, the most significant dimension of his motion-study photographs for
most of those who see them is, I would guess, not what the grids of images
reveal about the human and animal movements photographed, but the
relentlessness of the series in its graphic regularity and in its extent. Muybridge's system is more fully his subject than any particular information his
system was designed to reveal. The nakedness or near nakedness of Muybridge's subjects may have had a scientific function (it revealed the particulars of musculature in motion), but contemporary viewers are probably
more fascinated that a nineteenth-century photographer could devise a project for which so many Americans could be convinced to expose themselves.

Naked Spaces – Living Is Round is fully enough structured so that we can see that it is not systematic in any conventional filmic sense, and this refusal of systemization is precisely Trinh's point. For her, conventional movies, and traditional ethnographic films, are less revelations than systematic cultural impositions. The Muybridge grid is built into the camera mechanism, which has come to us after a considerable history as a tool in an assembly-line industry. To pretend that the camera, or the film experiences it is used to create, can be neutral with regard to the cultural practices of nonindustrialized cultural groups, or of any cultural groups, is at best naive. The inevitable tendency of the cinematic apparatus is to reform the daily and yearly "round" of living into a serialized set of rectangular frames. Trinh defies this tendency by making roundness the most pervasive motif in *Naked Spaces*. As the title suggests, roundness is evident throughout the film. It is evident in the shapes of women's naked bodies, of many African artifacts and living spaces, in the organization of people with regard to one another at work and at play, in the movements of Trinh around the places she films, and, to a degree, in the structure of the film, which begins and ends with a particular, circularly arranged dance in Senegal.

Trinh's response to the implicit tendencies of cinema technology and of the history of filmmaking that has confirmed them has been to redirect cinema toward poetry and especially music. In *Naked Spaces – Living Is Round,* Trinh "dances" with a range of African cultures, making movements with the camera and in the editing in response to the visual and auditory rhythms she sees and hears. At the conclusion of the film, we do not "know" any particular information, as we often feel we do after most ethnographic films. And we don't experience the resolution of a fantasized adventure, as we do in commercial entertainments set in Africa. What we do have is a sense of Trinh's perceptually and conceptually complex experience of moving among a series of distinct and fascinating cultures, and a deeper awareness of the narrow range of cultural exploration characteristic of so many of our conventional cinematic "adventures."

NOTES

1. The script of *Reassemblage* is available in *Camera Obscura*, nos. 13–14 (1985), pp. 104–11, and in Trinh's *Framer Framed* (New York: Routledge, 1992), pp. 95–105.
2. Interview with Trinh in Scott MacDonald, *A Critical Cinema 2* (Berkeley, CA: University of California Press, 1992), p. 364.

14
Yvonne Rainer
Journeys from Berlin/1971

Compared to *Naked Spaces – Living Is Round, Powaqqatsi,* and *The Carriage Trade,* Yvonne Rainer's *Journeys from Berlin/1971* may seem rather narrow geographically. The events depicted and referred to in the film take place primarily in industrialized sectors of Europe – specifically in Germany, England, and the Soviet Union – and in the United States (there are references to other locales: South Africa, Vietnam, Japan, etc.). And Rainer does not use the camera to document other cultures: *Journeys from Berlin/1971* is constructed largely of unconventional dramatic performances and recyclings of texts written by others. Nevertheless, the global resonance of the film is considerable because the issues it raises are global, because Rainer's sense of history allows viewers to traverse boundaries between then and now as well as between there and here (the same nation in different eras is, in a sense, different cultures), and because of her choice of Berlin as the geographic center of the film: No city has been a more compelling symbol of the collision and intermingling of different political systems and different cultures than Berlin was during the years between the construction and dismantling of the Wall.

Journeys from Berlin/1971 developed as the logical next step in an extended response to cinematic convention that began in 1967–8 with several short films, and continued through the features that followed.[1] *Film about a Woman Who...* (1974), in particular, was an early cinematic confrontation of what would come to be thought of as "the male gaze." While Rainer does explore the romantic and sexual lives of her characters, the characters are not conventionally beautiful or romantic; she refuses, even in scenes where sex is at issue, to provide viewers with erotic pleasure; and the narrative is conducted in an unusual self-reflexive manner that includes *tableaux vivants,* extensive printed texts, and still photographs. In some

instances, *Film about a Woman Who*... confronts the convention of the gaze quite directly. In one long, continuous shot, the camera reveals a naked woman with bloomers on the floor at her feet; while two women look on, a man (his eyes directed consistently at the camera) slowly pulls the bloomers up as the camera tracks closer, then veers to the left, to Rainer's face on which are affixed news clippings of Angela Davis's diary entries about her love affair with George Jackson. The issue of the voyeuristic spectator is confronted in two different ways: first, a woman's nakedness is *covered* as the camera tracks in (and the man in the scene looks at the audience, not at her body); then, viewers are reminded of one of many instances where the media-trained citizenry's attention was deflected from issues of race and class onto eroticism. The shot deals with the issue of voyeurism as it functions during our "private" experience as film viewers, then reveals the larger, political implications of the pattern.

Whereas *Film about a Woman Who*... confronts the cinematic oppression represented by the male gaze, *Kristina Talking Pictures* (1976) explores the more general issue of individual freedom versus systematic oppression. The film centers on Kristina, a character loosely based on Rainer, and her struggle to come to terms with such international issues as the Holocaust and the endangering of the environment by multinational corporations. It asks, How can a filmmaker deal progressively with systematic oppression on an international scale in a medium that seems to require that individual performers subvert their individual needs to the requirements of the artistic "system" instigated by the filmmaker? *Kristina Talking Pictures* demonstrates a range of alternatives to procedures that have allowed conventional directors to function, explicitly or implicitly, as bullies/dictators.

Rainer's quest for a nonexploitive cinema reached an apogee in *Journeys from Berlin/1971*, in which Rainer positioned herself about as far from the conventional cinema as it is possible to go – at least in one direction. Most commercial moviemaking is thoroughly dedicated to immediate sensual gratification and no concern can be allowed to interrupt this pleasure: In the long run, maximum profits must be made, so that the films' producers can themselves achieve the maximum possible sensual gratification in their own lives. As is true in her earlier features, *Journeys from Berlin/1971* does include narrative: Interesting stories are read on the soundtrack or are presented in printed texts. But Rainer forgoes entirely the sensual articulation of narrative standard in the commercial cinema. There are no ro-

Patient (Annette Michelson) and therapist; man and woman in Berlin; part of a mantelpiece, from Yvonne Rainer's *Journeys from Berlin/1971* (1979).

mantic conversations, no naked bodies, no erotic scenes, no chases, no choreographed violent moments. And, as if this were not enough, Rainer *also* ignores those alternative sensual pleasures (pleasures in the formal qualities of the image, for instance) exploited by other critical films. To put this another way, *Journeys from Berlin/1971* is about as unwatchable as a film can get... while still remaining interesting and thought-provoking.

Journeys from Berlin/1971 is structured similarly to Benning's *American Dreams* and Friedrich's *The Ties That Bind* (though, of course, it predates both): Rainer uses a variety of sources of information in both the imagery and on the soundtrack; each becomes a motif during the film's 125 minutes. *Journeys from Berlin/1971* begins with a conversation between a man (Vito Acconci) and a woman (Amy Taubin) on the soundtrack: The man has come home on a Friday evening, apparently after looking for work; he and the woman prepare dinner while they discuss, among other things, various social revolutionaries, many of them women. During the discussion, they read to each other from the revolutionaries' memoirs. Of course, the idea that a couple in a movie might actually enjoy such a discussion – that they might discuss something other than their romance – is a response to the narrow range of conversation typical of most conventional films and the resulting implication that the adults worth the attention of filmmakers never discuss politics, history, or philosophy, or use a relationship as a means of informing themselves.

Each of the film's other major motifs also confronts limitations of conventional cinema, either by focusing on issues usually considered too complex or "depressing" for the movies, or by using unusual, self-reflexive formal means that undercut standard assumptions about continuity. The first visual imagery – other than the printed credits – is a rolling text: "Let's begin somewhere. In 1950 a draft for a political criminal law in the Federal Republic of Germany contained the following sentence: 'The danger to the community comes from organized people.' "[2] During the remainder of the film Rainer periodically returns to this rolling text to develop the story of the Baader–Meinhof Gang (at various points during *Journeys from Berlin/ 1971*, the man and woman in the kitchen also discuss Baader and Meinhof), a group of German revolutionaries who carried out a series of violent responses to what they perceived as reactionary policies, and were ultimately captured and imprisoned. In 1976 and 1977 they were found dead in their cells; the authorities claimed it was suicide, but there was widespread suspicion that they had been murdered. A third narrative is introduced textually by the printed title, "April 27, 1951": a reading on the soundtrack of excerpts of an unidentified adolescent girl's diary in which the girl struggles to make sense of the relationship between her personal experiences and thoughts, and larger social and political struggles.

A fourth extended narrative motif, the most complex in the film, begins several minutes after these others are under way. The basic situation is an older woman (played by scholar/theorist Annette Michelson) talking with a psychotherapist. Their conversation ranges over many topics; it is full of references to what we assume are crucial moments in the woman's personal past, as well as to larger issues, including the political implications of psychotherapy itself. Near the end of the film, the patient reveals the events that surrounded her suicide attempt in 1971 in Berlin (hence the 1971 in the title), and about suicide in general.

Throughout the therapy sessions, Rainer interrupts the continuity of the visuals and of the sounds. The identity of the therapist changes – from woman to man to young boy – and as the patient's story develops, various "souvenirs" from it appear on the table between the patient and the therapist. In the background, a group of performers seen from different angles (actually they are seen in a mirror mounted behind the patient) perform various symbolic events that relate in different ways to what the patient and therapist are saying. Generally, these performances are suggestive of earlier Rainer films and the performance work out of which her original films developed. They are thus representations of Rainer's professional past (and, to the extent that her experiences as an artist developed out of her personal experiences, deflections of the personal past) *and* of the past of the character undergoing therapy. The verbal interchanges between the therapist and patient are also continually interrupted, so that we hear only excerpts of conversations and quotations. This motif is made all the more complex by the fact that the excerpts we *do* hear elide into one another to form a rather surreal stream of consciousness.

In addition to the four motifs that elaborate the stories of particular, identifiable people or characters, *Journeys from Berlin/1971* includes a variety of visual elements that, in one way or another, illuminate and obfuscate the major motifs. These visual elements include black-and-white aerial shots of Stonehenge; black-and-white aerial footage of the Berlin wall; color shots of a Berlin street through a third-floor apartment window, of a London intersection through a window, and of The Bowery in New York City through a window; imagery shot from a train moving through an industrial landscape, and from a car moving by drugstores in Berlin. There are also periodic, heavily edited, black-and-white passages of a woman (Cynthia Beatt) and man (Antonio Skarmeta) walking back and forth on a square in front of a strange and ornate, but unidentified building. There are several brief passages, seen once or twice, that involve other people: one woman (Rainer) having a recorder lesson; a young man (Rainer's brother) sitting in a chair near a fireplace with family memorabilia on the mantel; and, at the conclusion of the film, Rainer tearfully reading a letter that begins "Dear Mama."

Finally, periodic color tracking shots reveal a mantelpiece in close-up. The objects and photographs arranged on the mantelpiece are references to the stories conveyed during other parts of *Journey from Berlin/1971;* they create a form of symbolic montage within each of the continuous tracking shots. Mantelpieces are conventionally positions of honor in the home, where central artifacts of family life are displayed. Generally, the display is seen as specific to the particular family, private, apolitical. By including vestiges of the various events she's referred to on *her* mantelpiece, Rainer critiques this convention and the assumption it encodes: that private family life is somehow detached from the political and social realities of the world outside the home. The continuousness of the tracking shots that register the varied objects suggests that all the events they represent are parts of a single, evolving set of social/political conditions that viewers can either pretend to ignore, or engage.

Taken as a whole, *Journeys from Berlin/1971* demonstrates a multileveled critique of conventional cinema. As has been suggested, Rainer's use of a serial structure, and her refusal to supply any moments that titillate the conventional male gaze or even the general fascination with media stardom, interfere with conventional pleasure, as does her decision to raise complex issues without providing the viewer with a conventional sense of closure. Rainer's critique of the conventional and traditional (in both commercial and critical cinema) includes her refusal of almost any kind of tour de force. There is nothing notable about the imagery we see in *Journeys from Berlin/ 1971 except* its conceptual implications. I think it's fair to say that there is scarcely a moment of conventional visual beauty in the entire film. The pans along the mantelpiece are stately, the imagery during the therapy sessions is complex, but in terms of chiaroscuro, texture, design, and rhythm, Rainer's shots are relentlessly, and most likely purposely, uninteresting, even drab – the antithesis of *The Carriage Trade, Powaqqatsi, Naked Spaces – Living Is Round,* and nearly all the other films mentioned in this volume. Even in those instances where one might assume the visually spectacular could have been available – the aerial shots of Stonehenge, or even of the Berlin Wall, might have been breathtaking the way the early shots of landscape in *Koyaanisqatsi* are – it is refused. Similarly, although Rainer's overall structure is obviously thoughtful and precise, there is no attempt to engage

162

the viewer in the intricacy of the intersections between images, texts and sound. Rainer reveals that there *are* historical and ideological connections between the different sources of information included in *Journeys from Berlin/1971*, but without drawing undue attention to her own dexterity in providing the revelation.

Although the film withholds much of what viewers tend to expect, however, the stories told in the various printed and spoken texts are fascinating and often gripping. Particularly memorable are the excerpts from Alexander Berkman's *Prison Memoirs of an Anarchist* that detail his attempt to assassinate industrialist Henry Clay Frick on July 23, 1892; and from Vera Zasulich's description of her attempt to kill St. Petersburg police chief Trepov on July 24, 1877 (in retaliation for his having ordered the flogging of a political prisoner who had failed to remove his hat) — read, respectively, by "he" and "she" in the kitchen, as part of their discussion of political violence.

And the connections between layers of information in *Journeys from Berlin/1971* are often intriguing. At times a visual image serves as a metaphor for something we hear on the soundtrack. Immediately after the beginning of the kitchen conversation between the man and woman, the soundtrack cuts away to the voice of the young girl reading from an April 27, 1951, diary entry in which she puzzles about the powerful impact that certain obviously contrived melodramatic stories have had on her:

Yesterday I went to an assembly in 306. A girl sang "Come come, I love you truly" from *The Chocolate Soldier*. As she sang I began to feel the most peculiar sensations. Cold shivers were wracking my entire body. Clammy currents ran all over me. I thought I was sick, but when she had finished, the shivers left me. Very often these sensations come to me when I hear or read of some outstanding human experience of bravery or perseverance, or a story of great emotional appeal. Sometimes these stories are absolutely corny or excessively melodramatic, like the one Louise Utis told in Oral English the other day about a G.I. who corresponds with a girl whom he intends to marry as soon as he returns from the war. His face is left badly scarred and he is also crippled after a battle. The day before his ship is to dock in the U.S. the girl is hit by a car. She suffers a serious brain injury which results in blindness. There was some dramatic closing which I can't remember. At any rate, during the last few sentences I had the chills. I really fight against them because basically I reject such stories for their contrived nature and unreality. Intense drama is always so removed from my own life that it leaves me with an empty feeling. I was also irked by the melodramatic manner of delivery. . . . Then what in God's name do those damned shivers mean?

The girl's comments are juxtaposed with aerial footage of Stonehenge, suggesting a connection between the girl's puzzlement and the historical mystery of Stonehenge and our continued fascination with it. The juxtaposition also helps to foreshadow and account for the nature of *Journeys from Berlin/ 1971*, which does present "melodramatic" stories, but avoids fabricating them by recycling first-person narratives about real historical events, and eliminates nearly all vestiges of a conventional "melodramatic manner of delivery."

In other instances, soundtrack and visuals intersect in more literal ways. At one point, the couple cooking and talking in the kitchen receive an obscene phone call. The fact that we recognize the voice on the phone as that of the man in the kitchen (he phones the therapist in another instance) draws attention to the artifice of the film and, perhaps, to the potential of an individual to have one role in his social life and another in private life. The voice says "obscene" things like "Even Trotsky did it. . . . He said Stalin was always sulking." The woman hangs up and the two laugh at their being interrupted by a "heavy breather"; and *their* laughing on the soundtrack is juxtaposed with a shot of a laughing Cynthia Beatt in front of the ornate building in Berlin. In a sense, Beatt can join in the laughter because the usual woman-terrorizing lines are not said by this caller (or in this film). At the same time, although the idea of an anonymous phone caller saying political, rather than sexual, "obscenities" may be amusing, it is only amusing in a place where such political statements are not dangerous. And, conversely, this reversal of convention confirms the gender-political implications of sexually obscene phone calls: The callers harass women, regardless of whether the calls are received in real life or, indirectly, in the movie theater.

Later, as the man reads Berkman's description of his journey into industrial Pittsburgh, the visuals reveal a grim, industrial landscape seen through the window of a train – almost as though Berkman's journey is being dramatized by Rainer. That this current journey by train is a motif that begins early in the film and that the industrial landscape itself could be nearly anywhere suggests that the issues involved in Berkman's attempted assassination of Fricke not only remain important, but are the historical background for the industrialization that continues to transform the world – an idea emphasized formally by the fact that during this particular juxtaposition the train ride is for the first time seen in black and white. This use of black and white is in one sense conventional (in contemporary films, black and white often suggests the past) *and* a confrontation of the convention: Since it seems to be the *same* train trip, the implication is that the past is a not separate reality, but is part of our current "journey." Even the fact that Berkman's assassination attempt takes place in 1892 is suggestive: His journey is roughly contemporaneous with the development of the cinema technology that would soon allow viewers to meet the train arriving at the station in the Lumière film at the dawn of the film industry.

During *Journeys from Berlin/1971*, obvious connections between sound and image occur just frequently enough to alert viewers to the fact that, no doubt, there are connections they're missing, and, more importantly, to communicate a vision of the world engaged in a historically ongoing *global* struggle. As the film presents the histories of women and men whose experiences led them to forms of violent rebellion against their political and gender-political circumstances, the historical and geographical "distance" between these events and the present disappears, revealing parallels that

Yvonne Rainer addresses the camera at the conclusion of *Journeys from Berlin/ 1971.*

defy national boundaries and historical epochs, the most fundamental of which is their decision to sacrifice their personal lives for what they assume is a more progressive future. Viewers are challenged to consider what conditions might lead *them* out of the safety of their private lives into violent action: Would we be able to do what these women and men have done, even if circumstances did (do?) seem to demand it?

Rainer's own response to the complex issues raised in the stories she presents is implicit throughout *Journeys from Berlin/1971*. If we can say that the various violent acts that are recalled during the film (whether we call them "revolutionary" or "terrorist," of course, depends on our point of view) are attempts to subvert systems that exploit some people as a means of providing pleasure for others, then Rainer's decision to rebel against the cinematic conventions of the industry (and of previous critical cinema) can be seen as a parallel process. And the fact that the system she attacks clearly includes us (it is *our* pleasure she interrupts, after all) aligns us with those in the film whose tyranny and brutality "creates" rebellion. And yet, even on this level, things are not simple, as Rainer is well aware.

Journeys from Berlin/1971 grew out of Rainer's living in Berlin in 1976–7 on a fellowship from the German government. The first filming (of Beatt and Skarmeta in front of the strange building, of the recorder lesson, and of Rainer reading the letter to her mother) took place in Berlin, and one of the major motifs – that involving Meinhof and the Red Army – centers on Berlin. By the 1970s, Berlin had become a peculiar and fascinating symbol, the significance of which no visitor could fail to recognize. On one hand, the decision of the West German government to grant exemptions from otherwise compulsory military service to men who lived in Berlin (a piece of history Rainer explains at the beginning of the film) resulted in the city's becoming a haven for people interested in avoiding the regimentation and implicit politics of military service, and, ultimately, for an unusually broad range of artistic expression. On the other hand, the artistic and social freedom so evident in West Berlin functioned as powerful propaganda of the freedom of the West, as a compelling justification for the West's powerful military – even though much of what went on in West Berlin seemed as scandalous to many Westerners as it did to many East Germans who saw what went on there during visits or heard about it from others (or via radio and television). In any case, for several decades, visiting artists from many nations have joined Germans in keeping Berlin in the esthetic vanguard in film, in pop music, and in a variety of other areas. And Rainer's fellowship (and the frequent support the Germans have given to other American critical filmmakers) is an instance of this history.

166

Whereas West Berlin was, for a time at least, probably the wildest outpost of Western freedom of expression, East Berlin was its precise opposite. In few places in the world was the rigorous suppression of individual freedoms in the service of the state more obvious. The geographic division of the city also enforced a historical distinction. West Berlin was the epitome of the Modern, in both the positive and negative senses: It was a place of new esthetic forms, new fashions, new buildings *and* of angst, suicide (as the Patient mentions, "West Berlin has the highest suicide rate in the world"), pornography; East Berlin, on the other hand, was an old-fashioned industrial city that looked and felt like Western cities at the time of the Second World War. Whereas West Berlin has been almost entirely rebuilt (the destroyed Gedachtnis Church now stands as a tourist-attraction and symbol of what *was*), East Berlin still shows extensive scars from the bombing during World War II.

As many artists and commentators have recognized, the divided city of Berlin was a most compelling symbol of those political and psychic struggles with which many modern people are forced to concern themselves, as members of society and as individuals. The division of Berlin was both a symbol and an index of the division *between* capitalist and communist nations, of the debates that engage political factions *within* nations, and of our own schizophrenic thinking: We want freedom *and* control, old-fashioned values *and* modernity. The set of debates symbolized by Berlin is encapsulated in Rainer's film. In its production and in its consumption by viewers, *Journeys from Berlin/1971* dramatizes the paradoxical divisions of contemporary life – and of contemporary filmgoing. It is a film about radical politics that asks us (or at least allows us) to empathize with violent acts, even with terrorist groups, but it was dependent for financial support on funding sources provided by the very governments that have given the radicals reasons for revolutionary action. It is simultaneously a part of the "oppressive" system *and* of the response to oppression – regardless of how we determine which group is denoted by which term.

Journeys from Berlin/1971 is a thoroughly radical work of cinema that carefully refuses viewers many of the pleasures film consumers have been trained to expect. And yet, like other forms of critical cinema, its esthetic radicality is defined by the film industry: We can only define the radical in the context of the conventional. Our admiration of Rainer's rebellion is only possible because of our enjoyable experiences at commercial movies. Viewers of *Journeys from Berlin/1971* are thus simultaneously "freed" (from the limitations of conventional cinema, including its refusal to face the

167

complexities of the world) and "oppressed" (by the demands of Rainer's film and its rejection of pleasure).

Since completing *Journeys from Berlin/1971*, Rainer has continued to articulate her rebellion against cinematic convention. As the title suggests, *The Man Who Envied Women* (1985) returns to the issue of gender, as gender is depicted and used not only in conventional film history, but even by such quintessentially unconventional critical films as *Un Chien andalou*. *The Man Who Envied Women* reminds us that the Buñuel/Dali film partakes of the violence toward women implicit in so many commercial movies: The famous gesture of slicing the woman's eyeball may indeed represent an attack on conventional cinematic "sight," but in another sense it confirms the very structure it attacks – an irony (ironically) worthy of Buñuel himself. In *Privilege* (1990), Rainer explores a topic that, as a result of the gender construction of film history, has rarely been mentioned in conventional film: menopause. Whereas menopause has generally been seen as the extended moment when a woman's capacity for sexual pleasure (and a man's sexual pleasure in her) comes to an end – as a form of decay to be sympathized with – Rainer's film reveals the absurdity of such simplistic attitudes. The fact that *Privilege* is Rainer's most enjoyable and accessible film – the candid interviews, dramatizations, and texts she includes are fascinating, insightful, often good-humored; and the film is a pleasure to look at – is its most potent critical gesture: Instead of undermining conventional cinematic pleasure, as she does so effectively in *Journeys from Berlin/1971*, Rainer discovers pleasure where conventional and avant-garde cinema have been able to discover nothing at all.

NOTES

1. Like Yoko Ono and Michael Snow, Yvonne Rainer came to film having already established herself as an important contributor to the fine arts. Her influential career as a dancer/choreographer/performance artist is documented in *Work 1961–73* (New York: NYU and the Nova Scotia College of Art and Design, 1974).
2. The complete scripts of Rainer's first five features are available in *The Films of Yvonne Rainer* (Bloomington, IN: University of Indiana Press, 1989). The volume includes an introduction by B. Ruby Rich (Rich discusses Rainer's work up through *Journeys from Berlin/1971*), a discussion of *The Man Who Envied Women* by Bérénice Reynaud, and an interview with Mitchell Rosenbaum.

15
Peter Watkins
The Journey

As of this writing, Peter Watkins's *The Journey* may be the least known and least seen of all the films discussed at length in this book, especially in North America and England. But it is the most thoroughly global film of which I am aware. Indeed, it combines dimensions of all of the films discussed in Part 3 (as well as many elements of the films discussed in Parts 1 and 2), while extending their international implications into an entirely new form. Although *The Journey* was in many ways a novel undertaking even for Watkins, its relentless and thorough critique of commercial cinema (and mass media in general) is a recent addition to a filmmaking career that has been dedicated to confronting convention since the late 1950s, a career that predates all those discussed in previous chapters.[1] And, ironically, as unconventional as Watkins's career has been, it has from time to time been rewarded with accolades usually reserved for those most adept at avoiding serious critique, including an Academy Award.

Watkins is best known for *The War Game* (1965), a dramatization of the potential horrors of nuclear war. In the years since its controversial release (the BBC initially banned the film from television, and maintained the TV ban for more than twenty years), *The War Game* has become a widely influential "documentary," and it remains a film of considerable power. The irony is that the film's very effectiveness as a form of horrifying entertainment has obscured its critical insight. Although the subject of *The War Game* is nuclear war – the film dramatizes events leading up to a nuclear holocaust, the moment when the holocaust begins, and its seemingly unending aftermath – the focus of its critique is media convention: specifically, the "involvement" promoted by commercial media fiction and the "detachment," "objectivity," and seriousness of documentary film and television news. The passages in *The War Game* that look and feel most like

candid documentary – the sequences of people experiencing a nuclear detonation and its gruesome results – are acted fictions; and the passages that seem most ludicrous – a churchman explaining that one can learn to love the Bomb, "provided that it is clean and of a good family"; ordinary citizens revealing their utter ignorance about Strontium 90 – are either candid or based on real statements. *The War Game* foregrounds the fact that both entertainment films and documentaries are fabrications, the function of which is to maintain the system through which more products of both kinds can reach consumers. The central irony of *The War Game* is that its very potential to generate action resulted in its suppression by the BBC. Even the ultimate, grudging release of the film to theaters could not satisfy Watkins, since the only theaters that would show the film (at least in this country) were art theaters where the masses Watkins had hoped to reach did not go. *The War Game* escaped total suppression only to achieve art-ghettoization.

In the years immediately following *The War Game*, Watkins completed a series of feature films that, in one way or another, elaborated on the critique of mass media he had developed in *The War Game* and earlier films. The most notable of these are probably *Punishment Park* (1971), a psychodrama about early 1970s American political activism in relation to the Vietnam War, and *Edvard Munch* (1974), a carefully researched and unconventionally structured biography of the Norwegian expressionist. Watkins also saw many projects collapse because of his assumptions about how his work ought to function vis-à-vis the institutions that sponsored it. For most filmmakers and professionals in other areas as well, professionalism *means* developing the necessary skills to be accepted as an active member of an institutional system. One might disagree with one or another aspect of this system, and even try to change it, but, for most of us, the security available within the system seems necessary. Even in those areas of the film art world that define themselves as alternatives to the Hollywood industry, filmmakers, critics, exhibitors struggle to remain part of a systematic organizational framework, supported in large measure by government grants, art organizations, and institutions of higher learning. Like many artists and many avant-garde filmmakers, Watkins has remained suspicious of institutions. He has tended to put his suspicions into action by confronting the institutional limits placed on any project he has undertaken. Often, projects have not been able to sustain the pressure of this confrontation.

His final experience of this sort began in 1981, when he had generated

Three production stills of Peter Watkins directing scenes from *The Journey* (1987). Courtesy Sylvia de Swaan.

some interest in his returning to England to work on a remake of *The War Game*. Frank Allaun, a member of Parliament opposed to nuclear proliferation, invited Watkins to work with him in raising the necessary funding. London's Central Television agreed to cover behind-the-camera costs, and by spring of 1982 a production team had been organized, Watkins had scouted locations, and the production had been announced to peace groups in English cities. At this point, a modest remake seemed possible: The projected budget was between £100,000 and £150,000. For Watkins, however, the point was, precisely, *not* to work within the limits of what seemed possible, within the bounds of what the relevant institutions could comfortably sustain *with no fundamental change in the systems of which they were a part.* Instead, Watkins used the support he had gathered as a foundation on which to build a much more elaborate project, one that would use the making of the film as a means to develop new kinds of organizations for confronting the nuclear menace. Watkins began to build a network of support groups in cities throughout Great Britain; and the projected budget rose to a minimum of £500,000. Rather than take a chance on subverting their institutional security by committing their resources to a new, openly political process, the original sponsors of "The Nuclear War Film" backed away.

The collapse of "The Nuclear War Film" convinced Watkins that film- and television-production organizations were essentially so inflexible that there was no longer any point in trying to change them from the inside. The only route left was to prove that a major film on major international issues could be made without the assistance of any large production organization. Of course, independent filmmakers in North America, Europe, Japan, and elsewhere – including those discussed in previous chapters – have been working outside of formal production organizations for decades, and Watkins was aware of some of this work. But what he was about to attempt was well beyond the scope of the independent films he may have seen.

At the same time that Watkins was deciding to work independently, several commercial films and television shows were radically altering his understanding of the kind of film he should be making. Even as he was trying to arrange for a U.S. version of "The Nuclear War Film," Watkins was growing convinced that the process of dramatizing nuclear holocaust had become counterproductive: "What we must move away from now is the feeling that a nuclear war is inevitable," he said in November 1983, "To continue to dramatize the effects of nuclear holocaust can only serve a negative purpose now."[2] Especially in the wake of *The Day After* (obviously a watered-down version of *The War Game*), seeing more towns get blown away could only make people accept such sights as normal. The result was a challenging dilemma: How do you make a compelling film about the arms race and the many issues related to it *without* dramatizing a nuclear holocaust? The answer was determined, in large measure, by Watkins's belief that not only the finished film but the production process should function as models for the kind of progressive action necessary to change the global conditions that make nuclear holocaust a possibility.

The first stage of *The Journey* was to develop a production organization that was as independent as possible from major media organizations *and* from their ways of working with people and issues. This organization needed to be as fully international as possible, first because the issues Watkins was committed to exploring were international (he had come to feel that one of the weaknesses of *The War Game* was its focus on a single nation) and because one of the fundamental problems he had had in working with conventional media was its commitment to a parochial nationalism.

During the 1970s, in between filmmaking projects, Watkins had traveled – as many independent filmmakers do – through that network of arts organizations and institutions of higher learning that makes space available for alternative cinema. And like other filmmakers, Watkins had developed ongoing contacts with people in a variety of locations in North America, Europe, and Australia. Until 1982, Watkins had accepted these contacts as an alternative *exhibition* network, within which individual programmers were committed to a broader, often more openly politicized, exhibition schedule than commercial theaters or television. Watkins's first step was to confront this alternative network by asking individual programmers whether they felt they could commit themselves and at least some portion of their resources to the task of *producing* an alternative, global film.

By the end of 1983, Watkins had been able to organize a grass-roots, voluntary, international system committed to the production of an openly political film. Those who agreed to work with Watkins did so on the assumption that making what was now called "The Peace Film" would be a means for activating political ideas and feelings and for communicating beyond their normal circle of acquaintances and institutional affiliations – for "doing more" than they normally did. A local network formed in each location to raise money, to assemble a crew (insofar as possible, a *local* crew), and to arrange for local citizens to be the focus of interviews and community dramatizations – all in the hope of making contact, through Watkins, with people around the world. At this stage, *The Journey* had a good deal in common with the artist Christo's projects, which are fully as much about the redirection of community process in the name of art as they are about the finished products.[3]

Watkins's interest in activating local communities in the production of a global film proceeded from a recognition that, in the modern world, nearly every individual nation – indeed, every section of every nation, every city – is a mix of a wide range of racial and ethnic groups, each with its own heritage and identity. By arranging for the Hendricks family of Utica, New York, to enact an evacuation to Ilion, New York, as part of a larger community process, Watkins demonstrated not only the absurdity of federal government civil defense planning, but the degree to which government bureaucracies ignore the ethnic differences in the communities they make plans for. Nothing in the civil defense plans for Utica/Ilion confronts the fact that evacuating the African-American Hendricks family and their neighbors in a largely African-American and Hispanic city neighborhood to an all-white neighborhood in a much smaller city might cause problems for the evacuees and the host families. The *process* of dramatizing the evacuation scenes, however, did force those involved to come to grips, at least in a small way, with such issues, and to collaborate with people of other racial and ethnic heritages on a project with political implications for everyone involved. Basically, the community dramatizations were conceived as demonstrations of new, progressive uses of media in the service of multicultural community development.

At the directorial level Watkins's own process was analogous. His procedure differed from conventional media procedures both in the amount and the kind of work he proved himself willing to undertake. In fact, the "performance" of getting the film made was as spectacular as anything in the completed film. During 1983 and 1984 Watkins functioned continually as an international person. He organized and filmed in three American locations (Portland, Oregon; Seattle, Washington; and Utica/Ilion, New York), in the Hebrides Islands and Glasgow, Scotland; in France; West Germany; Norway; in the Soviet Union; in Mozambique; in at least two Japanese locations; in several Australian locations; on the Island of Tahiti (despite some French government resistance); and in two locations in Mexico. He did not travel protected by a personal or professional entourage; he moved from one nation to the next, from one language system to the next, alone, relying almost entirely on the good will of the people in the locales where he filmed.

When Watkins arrived at the National Film Board (NFB) of Canada early in 1985 to edit the film (the NFB had agreed to donate their postproduction facilities), he had shot over 100 hours of material, and, more important, had demonstrated that a filmmaker could interrogate contemporary systems not simply by working within them, but by moving across them, and finishing a complex, expensive project (*The Journey* cost the equivalent of more than $1,000,000). His individual achievement in seeing the film to completion was a way of demonstrating that all of us, whether we're involved in media or not, can and must do a good bit more than we tell ourselves we can do – if we care about delivering a more humane, progressive world to our descendants.

As a finished film, *The Journey* needs to be understood in at least two ways. First, it is an index of the production process I've just described. Even if *The Journey* were of no intrinsic interest whatsoever, one could hope that its redefinition of the filmmaker as *literal* circumnavigator of the globe (rather than as metaphoric circumnavigator, as in Frampton's *Magellan*) could have a considerable impact on a new, internationally minded generation of filmmakers, the way Warhol's rarely seen films have continued to influence the esthetics of alternative media artists. In fact, however, *The Journey* is by far the most interesting film Watkins has made.

The 14½ hours of *The Journey* are organized into an immense filmic weave that includes candid discussions with "ordinary people" from many countries; community dramatizations; a variety of forms of deconstructive analysis of conventional media practices; presentations of art works by others; portraits of people and places; and a wealth of specific information about the knot of contemporary issues that includes the world arms race and military expenditures in general, world hunger, the environment, gender politics, the relationship of the violent past and the present, and, especially, the role of the media and of modern educational systems with regard to international issues. Overall, the structure of *The Journey* has a good bit in common with the motif structures of *Journeys from Berlin/1971, The Carriage Trade, The Ties That Bind, American Dreams,* and even the second section of *Zorns Lemma,* though it is considerably more complex than any of these. Each major element in *The Journey* is divided into segments: As viewers experience the film they are exposed to the interplay between each individual segment and the surrounding visuals and sounds (nearly all of which are also individual segments of developing motifs), *and* they follow the progressive development of each individual element. Most important, each element included in the finished film functions as a critique of some dimension of the commercial cinema, or commercial media in general, by virtue of its content, its form, and/or the implicit process that was necessary to generate what the viewer sees and hears.

The particulars of *The Journey*'s structure can be clarified by returning to the Muybridge and Lumière models that have been so useful throughout this volume. From a very early point in *The Journey* project, it was clear that the central focus of the film would be a set of in-depth conversations with ordinary people about the current state of the world. The first priority in each major location was to find people (generally Watkins wanted families or family groups – parents and children of various ages) willing to talk with him about issues, on camera, for extended periods of time. These people were to be "amateurs" – people not accustomed to talking publicly, especially on film or videotape, about their politics. In the finished film Watkins presents each group with the same visual information and the same questions, and records their responses. His determination to raise the issue of nuclear holocaust without dramatizing one had taken the form of a set of photographs of the aftermath of Hiroshima and Nagasaki, which he presents to viewers early in *The Journey* and subsequently discusses with each family. The photographs are not unfamiliar, though the blow-ups Watkins uses with the families – and the inevitable "blow-up" provided by the movie projector – reveal the images in greater detail than one would ever experience seeing the images in conventional printed form (implicitly a critique of the miniaturizing and neutralizing tendencies of the print media and television). During Watkins's presentation of the imagery to viewers, the photographs are seen in a single, continuous, sync-sound shot, during which Watkins discusses specific details and the way each photographed instant fits into the larger tragedy of Hiroshima and Nagasaki – or, to put this into motion-study terminology – so that we are able to study the motion of this tragedy through extended meditations on a series of still images of it.

Similar formal principles underlie the film's presentation of the discussions with family groups. Basically, the Hiroshima/Nagasaki photographs, Watkins's predetermined concerns and questions, and his use of a similar setting in each culture (a room where each family normally gathered *as a family*), function as a grid against which the responses of the various groups of interviewees can be measured. This dimension of *The Journey* is experimental in a most basic sense. Some viewers of the film complain that Watkins's questions are boringly repetitive and the responses boringly predictable – especially after the first interview or two – but this is precisely the point: Confronted with the same basic evidence of the horrors suffered by men, women, and children under nuclear attack and the same questions about what is being done – in schools, in everyday lives – to ensure that similar events will not occur again, the Hendricks and the Crippens in the United States, the Vikans in Norway, and families in the Soviet Union, Scotland, Japan, Tahiti, Germany, and other countries around the world reveal the same discomfort with the photographs, with the fact that nothing is being done so far as they know, and with their own lack of information, awareness, and involvement.

But Watkins's experiment reveals more than what might be considered obvious; it reveals the discomfort experienced in most families at being face-to-face with such issues in each other's company. As deeply respectful of these people as Watkins is, he is also well aware that, despite the fact that they all might claim that the family is their most important commitment, they have done almost nothing, *as families,* either to educate each other about the international issues that affect their lives or to take action to move events in a progressive direction. For many of these people, the experience of being interviewed for *The Journey* was the first time they struggled as families with international issues, rather than "protecting" each other from the discomforts of reality, and the first time they collaborated with a media

Railroad tracks leading into nuclear submarine base, from *The Journey.* Courtesy Ken Nolley.

person to expand on a contemporary concern (rather than simply to watch the reduction of such concerns to tiny manageable bits by television news shows or newspaper stories). How they deal with the stress of this situation in the film – in their comments, in their body language, in their spoken and unspoken interchanges – is one of the central subjects of the interviews. Ultimately, the discussions are meant to function as role models. Their value depends on the degree to which viewers see in them a useful (though, at least at first, uncomfortable) activity they might instigate in their own homes.

The repetition in the interviews has another impact as well: It creates a set of expectations that are periodically surprised. By the time Watkins shows the Hiroshima/Nagasaki images to a women's farming collective in Mozambique, viewers have become so accustomed to the families' agreeing that the events recorded in the images were horrible and should never be allowed to happen again, that the Mozambique women's matter-of-fact statement that they see such things often and close to home, comes as something of a shock. What is a distant horror for most of the First World is everyday life for substantial portions of the Third World.

The actual filming of the family discussions was extended and private, and I would guess that no one except Watkins understood the depth of his commitment to them. In conventional documentaries, and even more so in standard news coverage, interviews are rigorously edited: The amount of recorded interview that finds its way into a finished film or news item is determined by the director's assumption about the usefulness or impact of what is said. This is especially the case when the interviewee is not an expert, the subject of the film, or a crucial witness to the actions of an "important" person: Interviews with the so-called man-on-the-street are usually little more than decoration. The focus of *The Journey,* however, *is* the thoughts and experiences of average people, and Watkins's commitment to the people who agreed to talk with him was nearly absolute: He was determined to provide an opportunity to respond to his questions and to treat the responses with respect, not simply in a metaphoric sense, but literally, in the overall allocation of screen time and in his use of continuous, unedited shots.[4] For those who had collaborated with Watkins in the production of *The Journey,* the biggest shock was the discovery that the completed film was 14½ hours long, and that an immense amount of screen time was devoted to the responses of the various families. Watkins's strategy is to place the audience in the position of listening to serious, real-time conversations with precisely the sort of people most people go to conventional movies *not* to see. At times, what is said is interesting; often it's boring, and sometimes pretentious. But viewers get a sense of who these people *are*. They are not *char-*

acters; they are people viewers grow to know. In Watkins's view, the film offers practice in doing the kind of listening necessary for building progressive local communities and a healthy world community.

In two cases – Norway and Utica/Ilion, New York – the families Watkins talks with are the foci of community dramatizations of scenarios made possible by current civil defense planning (in Australia, a third group of people dramatize, and subsequently discuss, the experience of being trapped in an air-raid shelter, and a group in Glasgow dramatizes the imposition of martial law). Although Watkins attempted to give these dramatizations the feel of reality (as he did so successfully in *The War Game*), they are always recognizable as dramatizations (sometimes the microphone boom is visible and there is other evidence of the production process); nevertheless, the impact of these activities on the people who enact them, especially on children, frequently develops a psychodramatic power as effective as a believable drama might create. A most obvious instance involves a group of Norwegian children, including Anne and Cornelia Vikan, dramatizing a terrified run to a bomb shelter. *Their* recognition of what could happen to them is more moving than any conventional dramatization of such an event I am aware of. Like the family discussions, the dramatizations are less interesting as film spectacle than as models of processes that could be developed by community groups, schools, and local media to assist people in informing themselves about the practical implications of current political and social policies.

Although the family discussions (and community dramatizations) are the central focus of *The Journey,* they are contextualized by a wide range of other kinds of information, nearly all of it developed by means of formal principles reminiscent of Muybridge and the Lumières: that is, in long continuous shots arranged serially in a motif structure throughout the film. *The Journey* is divided into eighteen approximately fifty-minute "chapters," separated from one another by question marks. This organization serves a variety of purposes, including the practical one of helping the film fit comfortably into conventional classroom situations. Within each fifty-minute chapter, the viewer sees segments of several interviews plus instances of at least four general types of contextualizing information: eyewitness accounts by survivors of World War II bombings; several forms of "guerilla reportage"; information in photographs, narration, and printed texts; and exquisite single-shot moments.

The most dramatic set of non-family-discussion motifs are the gripping eyewitness accounts of the bombings of Hiroshima and Hamburg offered by Tashiko Saeki, Hajime Hamada, Emma Biermann, and Werner Brasch. These survivors are clearly "experts" on man-made holocausts by dint of their personal experiences, but they are not the formal, "detached" experts conventionally used in documentaries. These people illuminate wartime disasters *and* the degree to which what they experienced continues to affect them: We can see it in their faces, hear it in their voices. And the fact that, as a result of the film's motif organization, we return to their stories again and again is a response to the tendency of conventional media to reduce painful stories to manageable units and to frame them in ways that defuse their impact.

The most extensive instance of guerilla reportage is the documentation by the support group in Montreal of the mass-media "coverage" of "The Shamrock Summit": the journey of Ronald Reagan to Quebec City in 1985 to meet with Brian Mulroney. The ostensible subjects of the meeting were Acid Rain and Canadian support for the deployment of additional American missiles in Canada. The Montreal group (led by filmmaker Peter Wintonick) filmed reporters – particularly from the Canadian Broadcasting Company – as they prepare for Reagan's arrival and as they participate in news conferences, photo opportunities, and other activities. By focusing on the summit as a media event, the Montreal group reveals the complacent "professional detachment" of the newspeople; their commitment to appearances, rather than to political realities; and the degree to which they are complicit with their governments in pretending that something of substance is occurring, when nearly all of Reagan and Mulroney's time – and of press energy – is spent on ceremonial occasions, particularly those that send implicit nationalistic and militaristic messages. The support group doesn't simply record the professional press's activities, however; they do what the official press failed to do: They interview members of the sizable protest against "Canada's" agreement to accept the American missiles and record the activities of the demonstrators. A second form of "guerilla reportage" was supplied by the White Train Monitoring Project, an informal group of Super-8 filmmakers who documented, phase by phase, the movement of the White Train carrying nuclear warheads from the Pantax assembly plant in Amarillo, Texas, to the nuclear submarine base in Bangor, Washington, and the local demonstrations against the train in communities through which the train passed. The Super-8 footage was reworked on an optical printer, so as to emphasize and visually interpret relevant details. It's arranged in the film in a manner reminiscent of the "replacement" images in *Zorns Lemma*; as the missiles near Bangor, the viewer nears the end of *The Journey*.

The implications of the various motifs I've been describing are regularly elaborated by photographs, narration, and printed text. Watkins's early presentation of the Hiroshima images has been mentioned; it is preceded by, and echoes, Bob Del Tredici's presentation of photographs from *At Work in the Fields of the Bomb* (originally a photo/text show, Del Tredici's images and commentary were published in 1987 by Douglas & McIntyre). Interspersed through many hours of *The Journey,* Del Tredici's images detail the production and deployment of nuclear weapons in America, revealing the mind-set inscribed in the production process itself and the attitudes of individuals directly involved. As is true with Watkins's presentation of the Hiroshima/Nagasaki photographs, Del Tredici's images are not shown in the conventional way, as if they are in a space detached from human interference; Del Tredici holds the photos, pointing with his finger at the details he describes – as if viewers are sitting at a table with him.

A variety of kinds of information are added to *The Journey* by an offscreen narrator (Watkins himself). Some viewers have complained that Watkins's use of this device betrays his loyalty to the conventional, Godlike (male) narrator critiqued by both Mulvey/Wollen and Trinh. But it is clear from the opening moments that Watkins is invoking the convention *and* critiquing it. *The Journey* begins with Watkins's voice; while the screen remains dark, he introduces himself:

> Well, hello. My name is Peter Watkins. I am English, an English filmmaker, at this time living in Sweden. And it will be my voice you will hear from time to time during *The Journey* as narrator. It's my intention to give you some additional information and also to comment on the process of the film. I do hope you will not feel that there is anything objective about the information I'll give you. Certainly, all of us working on *The Journey* have tried very hard with our research to make our information as accurate as possible, but I must emphasize that our presentation of the information *is* biased, due to our very strong feelings about the subject of this film.

Whereas the fact of a narrator introducing himself at the beginning of a film is not all that unusual (especially when the narrator is a celebrity or a well-known expert), it is nearly unheard of for a narrator to openly declare "bias," and to emphasize this bias in his tone of voice.

Watkins's particular British accent may seem, at least at first, to be a confirmation of the convention of the cultured British narrating voice, but it critiques this convention even as it recalls it. For one thing, the voice is not the usual professional performance voice: Like Trinh in *Reassemblage* and *Naked Spaces – Living Is Round,* Watkins speaks unaffectedly in his personal accent. Further, immediately after Watkins introduces himself, there is a pause (there is still no visual imagery), followed by the self-introductions of the two women who do the voice-over translations during the film. The women's offscreen voices have something of the impact of the offscreen women's voices in *Riddles of the Sphinx* and *Naked Spaces – Living Is Round;* they contextualize the conventional maleness of Watkins's narration. Further, as *The Journey* develops, we see Watkins *in* the imagery (most often, sitting with the families) and recognize his voice as part of the action in front of the camera, as well as offscreen. Or, to put this in terms of the "journey" motif so central to *The Journey* (and to this book), the narrator journeys *from* his conventional isolation in a spatial/temporal realm above and beyond the world captured in the frame, *into* the world of people whose struggles are the subject of the film; he journeys *from* detachment *to* engagement.

The Journey also makes extensive use of visual text. Periodically throughout the film Watkins presents textual information about the issues the film raises and about the film itself, using a variety of particular means – single question marks, words, declarative sentences and paragraphs, questions directed at the viewer, lists – and precise timing. In general, Watkins's texts – like Su Friedrich's – are more emotionally expressive than the comparatively cold, detached texts in conventional films; his timing humanizes the information the texts present, the way the hands pointing to details humanize the photographs.

The final type of contextualizing information is a series of moments of formal tour de force and exquisite beauty. Often, these moments serve to remind us of the many reasons why the world is worth struggling for and to reconfirm the degree to which those things we may find most lovely are endangered. In each instance, these moments are like films-within-the-film that can stand comparison with the single-shot films of Ono, Murphy, and Larry Gottheim. One of the most moving occurs during the final credit sequence. For sixty-two seconds, we watch a sleeping Polynesian child, in silence: The shot is a meditation on the real purpose of *The Journey* – a better world for the world's children – *and* a metaphor for the world's media viewership. All the beautiful moments that punctuate *The Journey* can be understood as critiques of the esthetic ideal of beauty – similar in goal but opposite in method to Rainer's avoidance of all conventional forms of sensual engagement in *Journeys from Berlin/1971.* Watkins's beautiful images demonstrate that to love the Beautiful in ignorance of the degree to which the beauty around us is currently endangered is to live an illusion: Cinematic beauty then becomes merely another avoidance of reality, a self-destructive fetish, rather than a catalyst for the maintenance of what we claim to love.

Although the 14½ hours of *The Journey* include a very wide range of imagery and sound – too many to fully document here – it is quite precisely structured. I have mentioned that, in general, the film is an immense weave – an epic version of motif structures evident in the other films discussed in this volume – but have not described the general contours of this structure. As has been suggested, many of the crucial strands of information are more-or-less evenly distributed throughout *The Journey*, though – as in Friedrich's *The Ties That Bind* and Trinh's *Naked Spaces – Living Is Round* – no element is deployed in a manner one could call rigorously systematic. For example, eyewitness accounts of World War II bombings are distributed about as evenly as any other information source, and yet this type of information has a recognizable and suggestive contour within the film: We begin with Ms. Saeki's account of her Hiroshima experience (Chapters 1, 2, 3, 6, and 7 include her reminiscences); the Hiroshima story continues in Mr. Hamada's memories (in Chapters 7, 8, 9, and 13) and in Mr. Shindo's (Chapters 12 and 13), as well as in the Mori family discussions and in the memories of the Korean, Jikkon Li. Whereas eyewitness accounts of the Hiroshima bombing tend to occur in the first half of *The Journey*, the second half explores the bombing of Hamburg, in Ms. Biermann's story (Chapters 8 and 18) and Mr. Brasch's (Chapters 8, 11 and 18). Viewers journey into the past with these people who describe their harrowing journeys around their devastated cities, *and*, as the film develops, "travel" from one side of the world to another.

The most crucial structural contour in *The Journey* is evident in the progress of the family discussions. Roughly speaking, each third of the film centers on a different family activity, and the arrangement of these overlapping activities is suggestive. During the first third of the film, Watkins engages the families in discussions about the Hiroshima/Nagasaki photographs, and to a lesser degree about the Del Tredici photographs and other information. The community dramatizations are a major focus during the second third of the film, beginning with the Vikans packing to evacuate in Chapter 6. The final third of *The Journey* focuses, increasingly, on the experiences and responses of the various families and other groups to seeing *Journey* participants from other parts of the world on television screens in their homes. The first instance of this procedure occurs in Chapter 15; by

Chapter 17 it is a major focus; and at the end of the film it provides considerable drama: The exchange of videotaped messages between the Smillie family in Dumbarton, Scotland, and the Kolosovs in Leningrad results, first, in Sam Smillie's flying to Leningrad to meet with Alexander Kolosov, then to a further exchange of tapes during which the developing friendship of the two men is obvious and the Kolosovs make plans to host the Smillie family in their home. Although all three kinds of family activity have to do with international issues, the change from one activity (and one use of media technology) to the next maps a progress in the direction of internationalism, *from* an inclusion of information about international events within the most intimate family interactions, *to* a movement of families out into the community to share experiences with other families and individuals, *to* exchange among "average" families in different parts of the world.

As is true in a number of the films discussed earlier in this volume, the most fundamental and pervasive structural dimension of *The Journey* is the network of interconnections among layers of image and sound. Early in the film, for example, when Watkins is introducing the coverage of the Shamrock Summit, he juxtaposes a visual of a Canadian newsperson (Francine Sebastien) doing a "topo" (news summary), with a voice-over translation of what Sebastien says: "Wrapped in a thick cloak of protocol and reception, the Mulroney–Reagan Summit has a full agenda. . . . " The image of Sebastien is framed so that, at first, she is seen surrounded by darkness – her face is visible through the space between a technician's arm and body: *She* is surrounded by a "thick coat" of *media* protocol and reception. In fact, the documentation of the topo reveals that the primary concern for Sebastien and those responsible for recording her is not the issues of the summit, but how she looks and sounds; the topo is redone several times, not to provide increased information, but to package the obvious more "professionally." This concern with appearance, with "cloaking" information in a specialized, elite language is not only parallel to the summit itself, it reveals how fully the commercial media is an arm of the governmental systems, functioning within the limited spaces and times determined by the government.

In many cases, the juxtapositions of layers of information at a particular moment are considerably more elaborate. The main title of *The Journey* is presented in Chapter 2: "The Journey" in different languages and colors rolls from right to left through the frame, accompanied at times by three layers of sound. One of these is Watkins's footsteps as he walks along the train tracks in the direction of the gates of the Bangor submarine base (this walk is a motif during much of the film); a second is the monotone of

Secretary of Defense Caspar Weinberger's voice listing the particular weapons systems currently under construction; and the third includes, first, a passage of a Tahitian chant introduced earlier in the film and, later, Watkins's identification of Weinberger.

This passage juxtaposes several forms of journey: The parade of titles from right to left is as consistent as is the sound of footsteps, the relentless weapons production process detailed by Weinberger, and the ritualistic rhythm of the chant. These parallel movements are variously interactive: The parade of different languages and the many nations they represent are, on one level, the opposite of the nationalistic impulse embodied in Weinberger's list, and on another level, a reminder that the weapons production process doesn't stop at the end of American assembly lines, but continues into other nations. Watkins's footsteps simultaneously reconfirm the step-by-step effort that was necessary to make *The Journey* and that is required to see it. The untranslated Tahitian chant represents the sorts of native languages and traditions militaristic forms of nationalism seem dedicated to eliminating, and since this chant has previously been heard in juxtaposition with imagery of Hiroshima and in connection with the issue of nuclear testing in the Pacific, its inclusion here also suggests the potential human costs of the policies Weinberger describes. A final implication lies in the juxtaposition of the chant and the ritualistic implications of Weinberger's listing of military hardware, which are emphasized by the specialized names of the various items currently in production.

Minute by minute, hour by hour, *The Journey* is conceptually dense in this way. The complexity of the film is easily missed, however, because of a conventional response to polemical film that seems shared by commercial moviegoers and serious students of cinema: *If* a film makes its ideological bias obvious, the convention suggests, *then* the film is simplistic, its message and style too obvious to be entertaining or worthy of study. Of course, the underlying assumption of this convention is that it is always more intelligent *not* to define a clear ideological position with regard to issues. Intelligence becomes a psychic space in which one can hide from reality, and the "best" cinema is inevitably that which most fully distracts viewers from the world, while simultaneously seeming to enlighten them about it.

The more fully one attends to *The Journey,* the more the coherence of its vision becomes apparent. At first, the film seems to jump abruptly from one place and time to another, but, by the end of the film, Watkins has made clear a belief that has been one of the foundations of all his work: that fundamentally, all places are simultaneously distinct *and* part of one place; all times are special *and* part of one time; all issues are important for themselves *and* as parts of a single, interlocking global issue. *The Journey* creates a cinematic space in which the viewer's consciousness circles the earth continually, explores particular families and places, and discovers how each detail ultimately suggests the entire context within which it has meaning. Like the other films in this section, but more fully than any of them, Watkins's film develops in the direction not of narrative climax and resolution, but of an expanded consciousness of the world.

Especially during *The Journey*'s first entry into the public arena as a finished film, Watkins was adamant that the complete film be screened. The film's length was primary evidence of Watkins's commitment to the issues confronted in the film and to the people he interviewed and collaborated with, and *these* commitments were meant to be understood as more central than his commitment to the comfort or enjoyment of those who would come across *The Journey* at film festivals: Those, in other words, who were fully enough parts of the media status quo to have the opportunity to indulge themselves in film entertainments for weeks at a time. The very idea that those who would commit to seeing *The Journey* would need to arrange their days around it was part of the film's central assumption: that to deliver a more humane world to our descendants we need to break out of our current, obsessive time schedules – modeled so effectively by the mass media and formal education – and begin rearranging our priorities and our days.

However, although Watkins was adamant that premieres of *The Journey* show the entire film, there is no reason to assume that *The Journey* always needs to be seen complete. Because of the film's serial structure, any particular chapter or set of chapters communicates a good deal about specific people, places, and issues *and* about the global nature of the film as a whole. In this sense, *The Journey* is related to modern poetic epics like William Wordsworth's *The Prelude* or Walt Whitman's *Leaves of Grass* in which any substantial excerpt can serve as an experience of the poet's vision *and* as an entry into an ongoing experience of the entire epic. Based on my experience using *The Journey* in classes and exhibiting it to public audiences, I would suggest that Chapter 8 may be the most effective single section to present, and that Chapters 1, 2, and 8 make a particularly effective feature-length presentation (indeed, on anonymous evaluations, my students have indicated that they find Chapters 1, 2, and 8 as powerful as any film experience they've had).

In any case, for Watkins, *The Journey* itself was as much potential catalyst as exemplary work. It was clear during the production process and it is clear as one watches the film that Watkins assumed that he was not simply creating a film, but a network of people who would find themselves part

186

of an international grassroots alliance that could function in a wide variety of ways: to produce and distribute this film and others, and to become involved in ongoing direct action. In *A Fable,* William Faulkner wonders at the fact that when the troops on the Western Front during World War I laid down their arms, left the trenches, and celebrated Christmas together in no-man's-land, they did not build on that moment of camaraderie and end war, once and for all. My guess is that Watkins hoped that *The Journey* might empower thousands of people to leave the systematic constraints in which they lived and begin creating a more fully international society. That this process has not occurred reveals that for all its sophistication as critique, *The Journey's* modeling of progressive media action and family relations has not been enough to inspire large-scale transformative change in those who collaborated on the film or in those who have seen it.

Although *The Journey* is the preeminent global film to date, it only begins to suggest the possibilities of a global approach. One can certainly imagine film projects that might effectively confront one important dimension of the Watkins film, and the other films discussed in this section, that reconfirms rather than critiques convention. Though *The Journey* involved thousands of people in many locations, one (white) man was in charge; the film is as fully a product of Watkins's vision as *No. 4 (Bottoms)* is of Ono's, or *Wavelength,* of Snow's. Of course, the very far-flung nature of Watkins's project almost necessitated that, no matter how open he was to the contributions of those he worked with, someone would need to maintain a firm grip on the process. Nevertheless, as Trinh might point out, Watkins's position as producer/director can be seen as a vestige of the very forces of imperialism and colonialism that have made new, progressive forms of cinema important. Of course, this limitation on the part of *The Journey* is shared by every film discussed in this section, including *Naked Spaces – Living Is Round:* That Trinh denies her directorship of the film does not mean that it was *cinematically* collaborative; *Naked Spaces* is, for all its critique of convention, *her* film.

There are any number of directions the urge toward global cinema might take. One is implied by the exchange of videotapes by the Smillies and the Kolosovs during the final reels of *The Journey:* Directors in various parts of the world could develop forms of collaborative interchange that would engage people of widely different cultures not only at all levels of production and within the finished film, but as distributors and exhibitors. Of course, as was suggested earlier in connection with Watkins's community dramatization, filmmakers could tap into the international vein simply by developing projects that would create productive interaction among various *intra-*

national groups. Watkins attempted to move in this direction in those segments of *The Journey* shot in upstate New York, and others have attempted to move in this direction. Indeed, one might argue that the interracial/ interethnic collaboration that produced Spike Lee's *Do the Right Thing* (1989) models an answer to the riot dramatized in that film. But for all the good work that has been done, we have a long journey to take before we can take pride in the way the cinema functions in, and around, the world.

NOTES

1. The best source of information about Watkins's career up through *Edvard Munch* is Joseph A. Gomez, *Peter Watkins* (Boston: Twayne, 1979). James M. Welsh's *Peter Watkins: A Guide to References and Resources* (Boston: G. K. Hall, 1986) reviews Watkins's career and provides a detailed filmography and an annotated listing of writings by and about Watkins.

2. Scott MacDonald, "The Nuclear War Film: Peter Watkins Interviewed," *The Independent*, vol. 7 (October 1984), p. 24.

3. My experiences working with the Utica/Ilion, NY, support group are detailed in Scott MacDonald, "The Means Justify the Ends," *Afterimage*, vol. 14 (April 1987), pp. 4–7. Ken Nolley was involved in both the Utica/Ilion shooting and in the Portland, Oregon, support group. See Nolley, "Making *The Journey* with Peter Watkins," *CineAction*, no. 12 (Spring 1988), pp. 60–71.

4. Watkins was to calculate later that the average length of a shot in *The Journey* was 45.9 seconds (as compared with 7.5 seconds in *The Birth of a Nation*, 4.4 seconds in *Triumph of the Will*, 3.6 in *Star Wars*, 2.9 in *Rambo 2*, and 11.2 in *The War Game*). This average is as high as it is because the shots of the interviews were as long as Watkins could make them, so as to avoid interrupting the spoken and/ or silent responses of the family members being recorded. Watkins's essay *"The Journey* – A Voyage of Discovery"* details his thinking. It is included in a special issue of *Willamette Journal of the Liberal Arts*, Supplemental Series No. 5 (1991), along with several assessments of *The Journey*.

Filmography

Distribution sources are listed at the end of each item, using the abbreviations and names listed below. In a few instances, films are available only from filmmakers, at archives, or from other distributors: Relevant addresses are included in individual listings. In a very few instances, I have not been able to locate distributors.

AFA (American Federation of Arts, 41 East 65th St., New York, NY 10021)
BFI (British Film Institute, 21 Stephen St., London W1P 1PL)
CC (Canyon Cinema, 2325 Third St., Suite 338, San Francisco, CA 94107)
CFDC (Canadian Filmmakers Distribution Centre, 67A Portland St., Toronto, Ont., M5V 2M9)
CS (Cecile Starr, 50 West 96th St., New York, NY 10025)
Circles (113 Roman Road, London E2)
Drift (83 Warren St., #5, New York, NY 10007–1057)
Facets (video only; 1517 W. Fullerton Ave., Chicago, IL 60614)
FMC (Film-makers' Cooperative, 175 Lexington Ave., New York, NY 10016)
Films Inc. (5547 N. Ravenswood Ave., Chicago, IL 60640–1199)
FR (First Run, 153 Waverly Place, New York, NY 10014)
Idera (2524 Cypress St., Vancouver, BC, V6J 3N2)
LC (Light Cone, 27 rue Louis-Braille, 75012 Paris)
LFC (London Film Makers' Co-op, 42 Gloucester Ave., London NW1)
MoMA (Museum of Modern Art, Circulating Film Program, 11 W. 53rd St., New York, NY 10019)
NY (New Yorker, 16 West 61st St., New York, NY 10023)
TWN (Third World Newsreel, 335 West 38th St., 5th Fl., New York, NY 10018)
WMM (Women Make Movies, 225 Lafayette St., Suite 207, New York, NY 10012)
Zeitgeist (247 Centre St., 2nd Fl., New York, NY 10013)

The Act of Seeing with One's Own Eyes: Stan Brakhage (U.S., 1971): CC, CFDC, FMC, LFC, MoMA
The Adventures of the Exquisite Corpse: Huge Pupils: see **Huge Pupils**
American Dreams: James Benning (U.S., 1984): CFDC, FR

Eureka: Ernie Gehr (U.S., 1974–9): CC, FMC, MoMA

Eyeblink: Yoko Ono (U.S., 1966): FMC (on **Fluxfilm Program**)

Film about a Woman Who...: Yvonne Rainer (U.S., 1974): BFI, CFDC, Facets, Zeitgeist

Film No. 5 (Smile): Yoko Ono (U.K., 1968): AFA

Flaming Creatures: Jack Smith (U.S., 1963): FMC

The Flicker: Tony Conrad (U.S., 1966): CC, FMC, LFC

Fluxfilm Program: many filmmakers (U.S., 1966): FMC

Fly: Yoko Ono (U.S., 1970): AFA

Fog Line: Larry Gottheim (U.S., 1970): CC, FMC

Friendly Witness: Warren Sonbert (U.S., 1989): CC, FMC

From the Pole to the Equator: Yervant Gianikian, Angela Ricci Lucchi (Italy, 1987): MoMA

Fuses: Carolee Schneemann (U.S., 1967): CC, FMC, LFC

Gently Down the Stream: Su Friedrich (U.S., 1982): CC, CFDC, Circles, Drift, FMC, LC, LFC, MoMA, WMM

Geography of the Body: Willard Maas (U.S., 1943): FMC

Gloria!: Hollis Frampton (U.S., 1979): FMC, LFC, MoMA

Go Go Go: Marie Menken (U.S., 1964): FMC

The Godfather, Part II: Francis Ford Coppola (U.S., 1974): Films Inc.

Hag in a Black Leather Jacket: John Waters (U.S., 1964)

Haircut: Andy Warhol (U.S., 1963): MoMA

Hapax Legomena (7 separate films): Hollis Frampton (U.S., 1971–2): FMC, LFC, MoMA

Heterodyne: Hollis Frampton (U.S., 1967): FMC, LFC

Highway Landscape: J. J. Murphy (U.S., 1972): CC, FMC, MoMA

The Honeymoon Killers: Vernon Castle (U.S., c. 1970)

Huge Pupils (Part I of **The Adventures of the Exquisite Corpse**): Andrew Noren (U.S., 1968, 1977): LFC, Noren (76 Cypress Lane, Aberdeen, NJ 07747)

In Progress: J. J. Murphy, Ed Small (U.S., 1972): CC, FMC

INGENIVM NOBIS IPSA PVELLA FECIT: Hollis Frampton (U.S., 1975): FMC

Jeux de reflets et de la vitesse (Plays of Reflections and Speed): Henri Chomette (France, 1925): LC

Joe and Maxi: Maxi Cohen (U.S., 1979): FR

The Journey: Peter Watkins (Canada..., 1987): CC, DEK (394 Euclid Ave., Toronto, Ont., M6G 2S9), Facets

Journeys from Berlin/1971: Yvonne Rainer (U.S., 1979): BFI, CFDC, Facets, Zeitgeist

Karagoez Catalogo 9.5: Yervant Gianikian, Angela Ricci Lucchi (Italy, 1981): MoMA

Kiss: Andy Warhol (U.S., 1963): MoMA

Kitch's Last Meal: Carolee Schneemann (U.S., 1973–8): Schneemann (437 Springtown Rd., New Paltz, NY 12561)

Koyaanisqatsi: Godfrey Reggio (U.S., 1983): NY

Kristina Talking Pictures: Yvonne Rainer (U.S., 1976): BFI, CFDC, Facets, MoMA, Zeitgeist

Last Year at Marienbad: Alain Resnais (France, 1961): Facets, NY

Little Stabs at Happiness: Ken Jacobs (U.S., 1959–63): FMC, LFC
Lost Lost Lost: Jonas Mekas (U.S., 1975): CFDC (partial), FMC
Magellan (many titles): see **Gloria!**
The Man Who Envied Women: Yvonne Rainer (U.S., 1985): CFDC, MoMA, Zeitgeist
Match: Yoko Ono (U.S., 1966): collection Anthology Film Archives (32–34 Second Ave., New York, NY 10003), as part of the Fluxus reels.
Maxwell's Demon: Hollis Frampton (U.S., 1968): FMC, LFC, MoMA
Medium Cool: Haskell Wexler (U.S., 1969): Films Inc.
Menkh (We): Artavazd Peleshyan (U.S.S.R., 1969): Pacific Film Archive (University Art Museum, Berkeley, CA 94720)
Mer Der (Our Century, also **Our Age):** Artavazd Peleshyan (U.S.S.R., 1982, 1990): Pacific Film Archive (University Art Museum, Berkeley, CA 94720)
Messiah of Evil (a.k.a. **Blood Virgin, The Second Coming):** Willard Huyck (U.S., shot 1971; released, 1975)
Morning: Ernie Gehr (U.S., 1968): CC, FMC, MoMA
A Movie: Bruce Conner (U.S., 1958): CC, LFC, MoMA
Musical Poster No. 1: Len Lye (U.K., 1939): LC, MoMA
Naked Spaces – Living Is Round: Trinh T. Minh-ha (U.S., 1985): Circles, Idera, MoMA, TWN, WMM
Nana, Mom, and Me: Amalie Rothschild (U.S., 1974): New Day (121 W. 27th St., Suite 902, New York, NY 10001)
New York Eye and Ear Control: Michael Snow (U.S., 1964): CC, CFDC, FMC, LFC, MoMA
No. 4: Yoko Ono (U.S., 1966): FMC (on **Fluxfilm Program**)
No. 4 (Bottoms): Yoko Ono (U.K., 1966): AFA
Opus No. 4: Walter Ruttmann (Germany, 1923): LC, MoMA
Opus No. 3: Walter Ruttmann (Germany, 1923): LC, MoMA
Opus No. 2: Walter Ruttmann (Germany, 1922), LC, MoMA
Organism: Hilary Harris (U.S., 1975): FMC
Palindrome: Hollis Frampton (U.S., 1969): FMC, LFC, MoMA
The Pawnbroker: Sidney Lumet (U.S., 1965): Facets
Penthesilea: Laura Mulvey, Peter Wollen (U.K., 1974): MoMA
Phi Phenomenon: Morgan Fisher (U.S., 1968): FMC
Plumb Line: Carolee Schneemann (U.S., 1971): CC, FMC, LFC, CS
Porter's Condensed Rituals (many titles): John Porter (Canada, 1968–Present): Porter (11 Dunbar Road, Toronto, Ont., M4W 2X5)
Potemkin: Sergei Eisenstein (U.S.S.R., 1925): MoMA, many others
Powaqqatsi: Godfrey Reggio (U.S., 1988): NY
Prince Ruperts Drops: Hollis Frampton (U.S., 1969): FMC, LFC, MoMA
Print Generation: J. J. Murphy (U.S., 1974): CC, FMC, MoMA
Privilege: Yvonne Rainer (U.S., 1990): Zeitgeist
Production Stills: Morgan Fisher (U.S., 1970): FMC, MoMA
Punishment Park: Peter Watkins (U.S., 1971): Joseph Gomez (Dept. of English, Box 8105, North Carolina State University, Raleigh, NC 27695)
Quick Billy: Bruce Baillie (U.S., 1967–70): CC, FMC, LFC
Raindance: Standish Lawder (U.S., 1972): CC, FMC

Rape: Yoko Ono (U.K., 1969): AFA
Ray Gun Virus: Paul Sharits (U.S., 1968): CC, CFDC, FMC, LC, LFC
Razor Blades: Paul Sharits (U.S., 1966): CC, FMC, LFC
Reassemblage: Trinh T. Minh-ha (U.S., 1982): Circles, Idera, LC, MoMA, WMM
Reminiscences of a Journey to Lithuania: Jonas Mekas (U.S., 1972): CC, Facets, FMC
Rhythmus 21: Hans Richter (Germany, 1921): FMC, MoMA
Rhythmus 23: Hans Richter (Germany, 1923): MoMA
Riddles of the Sphinx: Laura Mulvey, Peter Wollen (U.K., 1977): BFI, MoMA, New Cinema (75 Horner Ave., #1, Toronto, Ont., M8Z 4X5)
Rolls: 1971: Robert Huot (U.S., 1972): FMC
R-1. Ein Formspiel: Oskar Fishinger (Germany, c. 1927): MoMA
Roslyn Romance: Bruce Baillie (U.S., 1978), CC, FMC
Scenes from under Childhood, No. 1–4: Stan Brakhage (U.S., 1967–70): CC, CFDC (Part 1), LFC
Screening Room: Morgan Fisher (U.S., 1968): Fisher (1306C Princeton St., Santa Monica, CA 90404)
Seated Figures: Michael Snow (Canada, 1988): CC, CFDC, FMC, LFC
Serene Velocity: Ernie Gehr (U.S., 1970): CC, FMC, MoMA
Shutter: Taka Iimura (U.S., 1971): FMC, LFC
Sink or Swim: Su Friedrich (U.S., 1990): CC, CFDC, Drift, LC, LFC, MoMA, WMM
Sirius Remembered: Stan Brakhage (U.S., 1959): CC, FMC, LFC
Sleep: Andy Warhol (U.S., 1963): MoMA
Smoke: Joe Jones (U.S., 1966): FMC (in **Fluxfilm Program**)
So Is This: Michael Snow (Canada, 1983): CC, CFDC, FMC
Spirals: Oskar Fishinger (Germany, c. 1926): MoMA
Standard Gauge: Morgan Fisher (U.S., 1984): CC, FMC, MoMA
States: Hollis Frampton (U.S., 1967, 1970): FMC, LFC
The Student Nurses: Roger Corman (U.S., 1970)
Table: Ernie Gehr (U.S., 1976): CC, FMC, MoMA
Tarva Yeghaknere (The Seasons): Artavazd Peleshyan (U.S.S.R., 1975): Pacific Film Archive (University Art Museum, Berkeley, CA 94720)
The Text of Light: Stan Brakhage (U.S., 1974): CC, CFDC, LFC
Third One-Year Movie – 1972: Robert Huot (U.S., 1973): FMC
The Ties That Bind: Su Friedrich (U.S., 1984): CFDC, Drift, MoMA, WMM
Tom, Tom, the Piper's Son: Ken Jacobs (U.S., 1969–71): CFDC, FMC, LFC, MoMA
Trash: Paul Morrissey (U.S., 1970)
Tung: Bruce Baillie (U.S., 1966): CC, FMC, LFC
Turning Torso Drawdown: Robert Huot (U.S., 1971): FMC
Unsere Afrikareise (Our Trip to Africa): Peter Kubelka (Austria, 1966): FMC, LFC
Up Your Legs Forever: Yoko Ono (U.S., 1970): AFA
Viewmaster: George Griffin (U.S., 1976): CC, CFDC, MoMA
Walden: Jonas Mekas (U.S., 1969): FMC
The War Game: Peter Watkins (U.K., 1965): EmGee (6924 Canby Ave., Reseda, CA 91335), Facets, Films Inc.
Wavelength: Michael Snow (U.S., 1967): CC, CFDC, FMC, LFC, MoMA

Wax Experiments (many titles): Oskar Fischinger (Germany, 1921–6): LC, MoMA

The Wind Variations: Andrew Noren (U.S., 1968): Noren (76 Cypress Lane, Aberdeen, NJ 07747)

Window Water Baby Moving: Stan Brakhage (U.S., 1959): CC, CFDC, LFC, MoMA

A Woman's Touch: Warren Sonbert (U.S., 1983): CC, FMC

Word Movie/Fluxfilm: Paul Sharits (U.S., 1966): FMC, LFC

Zorns Lemma: Hollis Frampton (U.S., 1970): FMC, LFC, MoMA

Index

195